IS IT A HABIT OR AN ADDICTION?

The Step-By-Step System to Take Back Control and Gain Freedom

JUANITA SMITH

WHY NOT HAVE JUANITA SMITH AS A GUEST SPEAKER ON YOUR PODCAST, SEMINAR OR EVENT?

ACTIVATE HYPNOTHERAPY www.activatehypnotherapy.com.au

Tel: +61 416 209 724
Email: Juanita.activatehypnotherapy@gmail.com
Website: www.activatehypnotherapy.com.au

Juanita Smith is passionate about helping clients take back control of their lives. As a child, she was raised in an environment where addiction seemed normal. She experienced firsthand the emotional and physical toll that addiction has on families, health and longevity. As a specialist Clinical Hypnotherapist and Life Coach, Juanita has helped thousands of people with debilitating habits and addictions to find the freedom and control they really crave.

BOOKS BY JUANITA SMITH

IS IT A HABIT OR AN ADDICTION?
The Step-By-Step System to Take Back Control and Gain Freedom

Whether it's alcohol, drugs, food, gambling, cigarettes or something else, an addiction doesn't need to be a life sentence. This ground-breaking book is a must read for anyone who wants to take their power back. By following Juanita Smith's step-by-step system, FREEDOM is easier than you think.

ONLINE PROGRAM BY JUANITA SMITH
Advanced Stop Smoking and Vaping Masterclass

PRACTITIONER MENTORING GROUP WITH JUANITA SMITH
Advanced Stop Smoking and Vaping Mentoring Group

Other Books featuring Juanita Smith
Empowering Stories from Female Leaders Who Said YNot

www.activatehypnotherapy.com.au
www.isitahabitoranaddiction.com/resources

Copyright © 2020 Juanita Smith

IS IT A HABIT OR AN ADDICTION?

The Step-By-Step System to Take Back Control and Gain Freedom

JUANITA SMITH

Mind Potential Publishing

ALL RIGHTS RESERVED. No part of this book may be reproduced or transmitted in any form whatsoever, electronic, or mechanical, including photocopying, recording, or by any informational storage or retrieval system without the expressed written permission from the author and publisher.

Author: Juanita Smith
Title: Is it a Habit or An Addiction?
ISBN Paperback: 978-1-922380-06-7
ISBN Kindle: 978-1-922380-08-1

 A catalogue record for this book is available from the National Library of Australia

Category: Self Help Techniques | Psychology

Publisher: Mind Potential Publishing.
A division of Mind Design Centre Pty Ltd, PO Box 6094, Maroochydore BC. Queensland, Australia, 4558.
International Phone: +61 405 138 567
Australia Phone: 1300 664 544 www.thepotentialist.com
www.activatehypnotherapy.com.au |
www.isitahabitoranaddiction.com/resources

Cover design by: NGirl Design | www.ngirldesign.com.au

LIMITS OF LIABILITY | DISCLAIMER OF WARRANTY:
The author and publisher of this book have used their best efforts in preparing this material and they disclaim any warranties, (expressed or implied) for any particular purpose. The information presented in this publication is compiled from sources believed to be accurate at the time of printing, however the publisher assumes no responsibility for omissions or errors. The author and publisher shall not be held liable for any loss or other damages, including, but not limited to incidental, consequential, or any other.

This publication is not intended to replace or substitute medical or professional advice, the author and publisher disclaim any liability, loss or risk incurred as a direct or indirect consequence of the use of any content.

Mind Potential Publishing bears no responsibility for the accuracy of the information provided as either online or offline links contained in this publication. The use of links to websites does not constitute an endorsement by the publisher. The publisher assumes no liability for content or opinion expressed by the author. Opinions expressed by the Author do not represent the opinion of Mind Potential Publishing or Mind Design Centre Pty Ltd.

Printed in Australia

DEDICATION

To my mother, Natalie, who never realized there was a way to overcome her trauma and addictions, and who spent most of her 67 years alone.

CONTENTS

Foreword	1
Introduction	5
Chapter 1: Creating a Habit is a Feel-Good Thing	13
Chapter 2: Conscious Mind and Unconscious Urges and Cravings	19
Chapter 3: Reprogram Your Mind to Take Control	31
Chapter 4: Smoking – How to Quit	37
Chapter 5: Food – How to Have a Healthy Relationship	51
Chapter 6: Alcohol – When and How to Stop or Reduce	67
Chapter 7: Gambling – How to Take Back Control	79
Chapter 8: Drugs – How to Kick the Habit	97
Chapter 9: If Trauma Gets in the Way of Breaking a Habit or an Addiction	115
Chapter 10: What the Future Holds	121
Acknowledgments	145
References and Recommended Reading	146
Meet the Contributors	148
Meet the Author	151
What Others Have To Say…	153

FOREWORD

I've lived my life as both a good and a bad man.

I've been beaten, tortured and jailed, and addictions were part of my life for many years. Addiction, for me, was a symptom of my past - a coping mechanism that both saved my life and stole it too. It not only saved my life because it suppressed the things I didn't know how to cope with at the time but also stole my life because the addictions took away my freedom and, for a long time, hid my real strength.

I was fortunate, though. I felt destined for something more and somehow found my way through the past and out of the path of addiction. But I wish that I'd had the support of someone like Juanita Smith and the wisdom in her book when I was going through the thick of it all those years ago. I'm glad there are people like Juanita who help those who need it now.

I wrote in my book, *Born to Fight*, about growing up in South Auckland, New Zealand, in a life where we were as hungry as street dogs. Dad would beat us for any little thing. Fists, feet, broom handles, sticks, electrical cords - anything he could get his hands on.

My sister, Victoria, didn't get the beatings that my brothers and I did, and we used to think that wasn't fair. We knew something odd was happening, though, because dad would take her into a room by herself. We'd wait for the sounds of a beating, but those sounds never came. What we didn't know at the time was that Dad was putting Victoria through a very different kind of torture in that terrible room.

FOREWORD

I consider myself the lucky one. For years, I hid my childhood wounds in addictions - it was my coping mechanism - but that childhood broke my two brothers.

John, my second eldest brother, committed suicide in 2014. My eldest brother, Steve, his brain just snapped at some point in all the pain. He was lost to us at sixteen, in and out of psychiatric hospitals and he became a homeless schizophrenic. Thankfully, my sister, Victoria, sought help and worked to heal and get on with her life.

That kind of upbringing and early part of my life would have ruined many, like it did my brothers. Through resilience, strength and the power of the mind, I have gone on to achieve unprecedented success in my UFC career and personal life.

If I'd met someone like Juanita Smith, who also grew up in a life surrounded by addiction and came to understand its hardships intimately, perhaps breaking free of addiction sooner would have been possible for me too.

If I'd met someone like Juanita Smith, who also grew up in a life surrounded by addiction and came to understand its hardships intimately, perhaps breaking free of addiction sooner would have been possible for me too. Our mind is incredible; it can trick us into finding relief with alcohol, drugs and even tobacco and gambling, but Juanita Smith understands that pattern and helps people take their power back.

For me, I avoided life by using alcohol, drugs, tobacco and gambling. For others, addiction takes on many different forms.

When someone like Juanita comes into your life, I'd recommend you take a leap of faith and grab their help!

It took a long time before I dug my way out of the past, but I consider myself one of the lucky ones. Maybe it's time to let someone like Juanita show you how your mind can also be your best friend, once you learn how to take control of it.

I've learned you're not alone and there are people like Juanita Smith who understand how hard addiction feels and, surprisingly, how easy it is to get your life back when you have the right tools and help. Take a chance on your life again. Read this book.

Mark "Super Samoan" Hunt
Best-selling author of *Born to Fight*, and UFC champion (the real-life Rocky)

INTRODUCTION

It begins as a sticky seed embedding itself into a branch high up in the tree's canopy. The young strangler fig grows over time, being supported by the host tree, and once it establishes itself, its roots stretch firmly into the ground.

It's not long before several roots become grafted together, tightening the grip on their host, strangling the trunk in a latticework that constricts life-force out of the tree… feeding off its strength, until there is nothing left of the tree but the fig itself.

Addiction is the same. An addiction takes hold, it strangles the essence of you (the host), taking control of who you think you are – and before long, you become the kind of person who …

- Smokes
- Drinks
- Takes drugs
- Gambles
- Overeats
- Or any other habit or addiction

A story of addiction

By the time I was born, my mother was so traumatized by her life that she would be found passed out on the floor after taking copious amounts of Valium. She would leave my seven-year-old brother, Terry, to care for his new baby sister… me.

Plunged into the depths of her despair and coming from a genetic line of addiction and trauma, my mother's coping mechanism was cigarettes, prescription drugs and oblivion. It was little wonder

INTRODUCTION

that she didn't notice how ill I was in my early years. In fact, my brother and I were taken and put into a home when I was about 2.

My mother was a heavy smoker. She didn't want to smoke but she didn't have the skills or the will to stop. In fact, she gave up trying to quit.

My mother wasn't the only victim in our family to die from a smoking-related illness or trauma-related addiction.

There are many people, like my mother, who don't want to smoke, don't want to keep the habits or addictions they have developed, but do not have the skills or support they need to realize there are steps they can take to free themselves.

This book not only addresses habits, like smoking, but also provides tailored solutions to other common addictions, like alcohol, food, gambling and drugs. Whether you are personally affected by these or other addictions or are someone who helps or supports others to break free, within these pages you will find a step-by-step system to help guide you through the process.

All of these habits and addictions can be conquered when you know how.

My story

As a tiny baby, being looked after by my seven-year-old brother, I suffered severe ear infections that led to a complete loss of hearing in one ear and permanent damage in the other.

A major contributing factor to this ill health was passively inhaling 40 cigarettes per day from the time I was in utero until I was two years old and placed into a home. It wouldn't have helped that I was unable to sleep as a newborn baby, presumably due to copious amounts of coffee, painkillers and other prescribed medication that my mother consumed during her pregnancy with me.

Growing up in 1940s and 1950s New Zealand, my mother was a victim of the New Zealand social welfare system. She had grown up enduring physical, mental and sexual abuse. My dear mother was highly intelligent, had an incredible imagination and was acutely sensitive.

As a young adult, she wasn't coping with her life and the solution in those days was shock treatment.

Ultimately, my mother spent most of her life completely alone with cigarettes as her only companion, until she passed away in a psychiatric rest home at the age of 67.

Coincidentally, my cousin Shayne, a musician from New Zealand's *Straitjacket Fits* and *Dimmer* fame, published his autobiography in 2019 that chronicled our family history.

Shayne writes about our Grandfather Bob. *Bob was violent, and he beat his wife and children. My mum's oldest sister, Helen, remembers Bob's horse whip, and the boots he was wearing when he kicked her, the heavy, worn, thick leather ones with metal on the front. Some evenings, Bob would gather his girls around for fireside chats, and he would tell them about his own floggings from his father, where his father tied him upside down by his ankles and flailed him with a whip.*

These tales were related like ordinary family events, like a picnic, or a school ceremony, or a day out at the races. Bob was from a series of redeemers who had earned the right to put his own mark on his children's backs.

INTRODUCTION

From the age of two until I was 11, I was raised by my paternal grandparents but, when my grandfather passed away, my grandmother was too elderly to look after me and I went to live with my father. Unfortunately, this was frequently an abusive environment and, consequently, Shayne's mother, my Aunty Ricci, took me in from the age of 14.

Aunty Ricci battled with her own alcohol addiction too. For my family, trauma and addiction spread from person to person, generation to generation. For those who didn't find their way out, it was an abyss of dysfunction and pain.

Perhaps experiencing poverty, trauma and the hornet's nest of addiction at such a young age is what drew me to work with people to help them overcome their addictions and underlying trauma.

I often wonder what might have been different if only my mother and Aunty Ricci could have had someone in their life with my skills back then. Who knows - it could have been different for them and for us as a family?

This book is not only a culmination of the experience and training I have in helping others to overcome addictions and habits but also a testament of survival for those whose lives are affected by other people's addictions *too*.

The book lays out a simple step-by-step system that is highly effective when working to overcome these challenges.

If you personally want to break free from the negative impacts that poor relationships to food, cigarettes, drugs, gambling and other addictions have, this book is for you.

Also, if you are helping a loved one, or if you want to expand your tool kit as a practitioner, this system is tried and tested. It works.

By the time someone finds this book or finds their way to my clinical practice, they have often attempted many methods to break free of unrelenting habits and addictions. When they finally discover how easy it is to become free as a result of the tools and guidance I provide, they often wish they'd known sooner how simple it can actually be.

You'll understand that what you've been led to believe was an addiction is actually your brain's habit. I can teach your brain and your conscious will to break free from these habits and 'addictions' forever.

It was many years after my mother's battle ended that it dawned on me, as I treated yet another client who was struggling to break free from a common addictive habit, that my mother had indeed felt powerless.

And it's not only cigarettes or prescription medication that people feel controlled by and powerless to quit. Over the years, I have treated thousands for addictions to food, all manner of drugs, alcohol and gambling. Each of these topics are addressed in this book.

◇◇

Stopping addictions and habits is my thing!

◇◇

You could say it's because of my mum, or even Aunty Ricci. You could say it's because I chose a different path from other members of my family. You could say I ended up here for many other reasons. It doesn't matter to me why. What matters is I love

watching a client transform from feeling powerless to feeling empowered and alive again.

Throughout this book, I refer to the 5-Step System that I follow for a successful treatment.

Habits and Addictions 5-Step System

Step 1: Discovery
Step 2: Decision Point
Step 3: Expectations During and After Treatment
Step 4: Treatment
Step 5: Post Treatment (How to stay free and in control forever.)

In the book, I've provided many real-life stories of those who have recovered and are now living free of the substances or habits that controlled them for many years. I've outlined their stories and the steps I used to help each individual.

Throughout the book, I have also interviewed experts who work in a variety of specialty areas, such as drug and alcohol recovery. I did this to provide you with as many opportunities to break free as I could.

Before we get into the individual topics of food, drugs, cigarettes, gambling and alcohol, I begin this book in the same way I do with my clients in a clinical environment. I want to lay the foundation of change by educating your conscious mind too.

When you understand the layers of your mind that are involved in attraction to and recovery from habits and addictions, when you get why your brain can't seem to fight that 'stuff', then you have a better chance of supporting yourself, your loved ones or your patients to fully recover.

In Chapter 1, I tap into the 'feel-good' factor. Understanding this aspect of your attraction and frustration with the substance or habit, and the realization of why this is a habit and not an addiction, makes the first step to becoming free easier.

The answer is: It's an Addiction to the Habit, no matter what substance, no matter the choice of 'poison' being used. Be it gambling, cigarettes, alcohol, food and even drugs, it's a habit, and I know how to break a habit, and so will you by the end of this book.

Juanita Smith

CHAPTER 1
Creating a Habit is a Feel-Good Thing

BASE jumping is the most dangerous sport in the world. The risk of death is one to every 2,317 jumps. There are currently around 2,000 BASE jumpers in the world and 383 deaths have occurred since 1981.

Jumpers will jump from 148 meters or less, which is only half the height of the Eiffel Tower! They will jump from buildings, antennas, bridges and cliffs. These thrill-seekers are often people who begin with sky diving and then look for the next level of anticipation, the next endorphin hit.

A sky diver on the other hand, falls out of the sky at 10,000 feet, which is the height of 27 Empire State Buildings on top of one another! Because sky diving is done from a great height, statistically it's quite safe, you have far more time to deal with unlikely issues. However, with BASE jumping you have three seconds after you jump to open your parachute before you hit the ground.

BASE jumpers are fully aware of the risks - that's part of the anticipation. They know if there is a problem with the jump, there is a great possibility that they will either be left seriously injured or dead (usually death is the outcome).

Knowing the risks, they jump anyway because it is the most anticipated and exhilarating experience of their life.

CHAPTER 1: CREATING A HABIT IS A FEEL-GOOD THING

For the BASE jumper whose brain has become addicted to the rush of endorphins, the anticipation of the jump and the desire for the rush, far outweigh the risk. It's the ULTIMATE feel-good thing.

This might be an example of an extreme attachment to feeling good. However, the same principle applies to any habit or addiction. The BASE jumper knows they have three seconds to experience the endorphin rush, the person who is addicted to a substance or habit has a daily anticipation that strangles their individuality and will.

How it begins

When you were very small and learnt to walk, it seemed extremely difficult at first. If you've observed a baby since then, you've seen them teeter and totter, fall and crawl, till they get it right.

Just like any baby, you too started by crawling, bottom shuffling, even dragging your body around, but then came the point when you attempted to stand. Perhaps you were staring at your feet, a little confused about how to make them work. After a while, you moved a foot forward and when the second foot had no idea what to do, you fell.

But then you got up and tried again, you even fell over again but, after practice and perseverance, you finally took your first real steps, tentatively at first, then you were off and running.

Now when you walk anywhere, you don't have to think about how to put one foot in front of the other foot. It's simply something you do on autopilot. Similarly, if you've ever learned to drive a car, after practice, you don't have to concentrate on changing gears or how much pressure you need to apply to the brakes to stop at a traffic light. It's now something you do on autopilot.

Putting one foot in front of the other or driving a car is now programmed in your unconscious mind as an automated habit. You repeatedly practiced something over and over and now you do it on autopilot.

Similarly, when you create any other automated habit at the unconscious level of your mind, you create it because you repeat that action over and over again.

when you create any other automated habit at the unconscious level of your mind, you create it because you repeat that action over and over again.

Every time you take that action, your unconscious mind experiences a reinforced positive effect. The action of the habit is proof enough to the unconscious processes that the habit is within the 'safe and comfortable zone' and a positive chemical that makes you feel good reinforces to the brain that all is right with the world.

For example, eating a block of chocolate in front of the television tastes good and feels nurturing, perhaps even secretive if it's become a 'me time' thing. Alcohol and drugs may make you feel more relaxed, perhaps more confident, and provide your brain with a high or, if stressed, relief and a comfortable, mellow 'low.'

With gambling, your unconscious becomes attached to the comfort zone of the thrill of possibly winning and even the 'comfort zone' of inevitability and acceptance when you lose. Consciously, gamblers might not like the 'losing' part, but your unconscious is addicted to the habit of the rollercoaster of emotions.

CHAPTER 1: CREATING A HABIT IS A FEEL-GOOD THING

Often for a gambler, there is not only the thrill of the win but also a sense of resignation, almost relief, when the money is gone too. I've often heard a gambler say, "I love the thrill of winning, but sometimes I feel this sense of relief too, when there's no more in the pot to spend."

With cigarettes, it can often be the comfort of connection with others or an attachment to how they perceive smoking to look (e.g. cool). It can be as simple as the unconscious satisfaction of 'busyness', something to fill in the time or to keep your hands busy.

What's important to remember is it doesn't matter what the habit is or the substance used - if your unconscious mind didn't receive its perceived outcome from the action, then you wouldn't repeat the habit or the habits would be far easier to stop.

Every time you do the habit, or surrender to the urge or craving, you reinforce that pattern, and the effect to your unconscious mind provides more evidence that you need to do it again. Your unconscious mind then associates the chemical high or low with that behavior and the desire for that chemical high or low becomes the trigger for the habit.

When I was a teenager, alcohol made me feel more relaxed and confident. It numbed the pain of rejection and abandonment and it covered up my self-doubt and nervousness.

Over the next 20 years, a great part of my life was fueled by alcohol. Even as a young mum, a couple of glasses of wine at the end of a stressful day with my tiny offspring was not unusual. Many friends and colleagues tell a similar story.

Throughout those years, alcohol became my feel-good thing. I could have easily gone down the path of addiction and destruction, but I didn't. A part of me wanted to surrender to it, but another part always wanted something more for myself. You'll read more about the 'decision point', the tipping point that changed the course of my life in the final Chapter about

> So, what is it within each of us that determines whether or not we continue down a destructive path, chasing the feel-good thing? What made me be able to say no to that path, yet my mother and aunt couldn't or didn't succeed? Why is it that so many others in the world try again and again to gain freedom from addictions… but slip back and lose control again when stressed?
>
> These are just some of the many questions that will be answered in this book.

In Chapter 2, I'll begin to answer those questions and delve deeper into the unconscious and conscious desires, the triggers and patterns that need to be changed, in order to help align your conscious awareness with the desire to take a different path, to let go of the addiction to the habit.

CHAPTER 2

Conscious Mind and Unconscious Urges and Cravings

When someone tries to quit an unwanted habit by using willpower, using just the conscious mind, they are often triggered, causing them to fall back into the old habit.

Only 12% of smokers can manage to quit using willpower 'cold turkey.' Some of those who achieve freedom from the habit through sheer willpower, still describe experiencing cravings for many years after they last smoked a cigarette.

Alcoholics Anonymous (or AA, as it is most frequently known) has more than 115,000 groups worldwide. Lance Dodes, a retired Harvard Medical School psychiatry professor, wrote *The Sober Truth: Debunking the Bad Science Behind 12-Step Programs and the Rehab Industry*. In his book, he states AA's success rate is somewhere between 5% and 8%, based on the data from AA's retention rates, sobriety and active involvement.

Gamblers Anonymous reports an 8% success rate for members after one year.

Similar statistics are reported for food addictions and drugs.

Why are the numbers so low across the board for addicts who try to stop unwanted habits? It is because the addiction is out of their control. It is an unconscious behavior programmed in their unconscious mind.

A person tries to stop but gives in to the overwhelming urge to do the habit, especially in stressful circumstances or during habitual times and event triggers. Most methods to quit rely on willpower, and willpower cannot compete with the programming in the unconscious mind.

Withdrawals

People describe the 'withdrawals' from a habit as feeling irritable, emotional, breaking out in a cold sweat, sleepless, stressful thinking patterns, and other feelings and emotions that make them feel like it's too difficult. The common term I hear is that they give up and give in to the pressure to do the habit again. Often, after multiple attempts to change, they surrender to the habit which feels almost tangible.

For smokers, when this happens, they tend to blame it on nicotine addiction. They've been led to believe how addictive nicotine is. It's a good 'fall back' because it's the only thing that can explain why they are feeling so many physical and emotional responses.

If this is the case, how do you explain the overwhelming urge to gamble on the slot or poker machines? Nicotine is an external chemical, so it's understandable to believe it's the craving for the loss of the chemical that's causing the problem. But, in the case of gamblers, for instance, they don't breathe in an external chemical when they gamble. If it's the external chemical addiction that causes you to fail at quitting something, why doesn't a gambler find it easier to quit? There's no external chemical involved.

The truth is, in the majority of cases involving external chemicals such as nicotine, drugs and food, the urge for the habit stems from a psychological impulse.

> *The impulse manifests into an emotional or physical reaction in the body, it is interpreted as a craving or withdrawal symptom.*

When someone has an addiction to a habit and tries to abstain, they get an overwhelming and sometimes tangible sensation they call an urge or craving when triggered to do the habit.

This tangible sensation, or thought process, is actually their unconscious mind trying to remind them that they need to do the habit. Their brain is 'tricking' them into thinking they need the external substance or behavior when, in fact, it wants the 'chemical rush' that habit produces *internally*.

You are not addicted to the external substance or behavior. Your brain is programmed to want the 'comfort' of the pattern it remembers to trigger the release of internal feel-good hormones.

Why does the unconscious mind continue to trick you this way?

Your unconscious mind is your survival mechanism. Its role is to protect you and keep you safe. If it has learned that eating a big bag of potato chips made you feel nurtured at some point in your past, the unconscious now equates that feeling of security with potato chips and thinks they are imperative to stay alive.

If you resist eating those crisps, then your unconscious will trigger all manner of physical reactions in your body or thought patterns to remind you physically and emotionally that you are 'not safe' until you eat.

CHAPTER 2: CONSCIOUS MIND AND UNCONSCIOUS URGES AND CRAVINGS

Your unconscious mind controls up to 95% of your impulses and habits, your thought patterns and emotional reactions. It controls trillions of internal processes that occur every minute of every day which you don't need to think about. Your breathing happens whether you're focused on it or not, your heart keeps pumping, and your digestive system processes food - all of these happen unconsciously to keep you alive. When the unconscious is programmed with repetition, it can learn new patterns – for example, driving a car, reaching for an impulse buy in the chocolate aisle at the supermarket, hunger pangs, and, yes, emotional and physical impulses to do that addiction to the habit again and again.

Your unconscious is many thousands of times more powerful than your conscious thinking or willpower. Whatever has been programmed at the unconscious level becomes the blueprint of who you think you are, the blueprint of your habits and reactions to the world.

If that blueprint moves you toward your desired conscious outcomes, then everything is aligned and you get what you want. If, however, that blueprint is programmed by an earlier repetitive habit and you now want to change that pattern, the unconscious is now out of alignment because of your conscious decision to change a habit.

Internally you are at war with your blueprint for survival.

Everything you have experienced in your entire life, right back to the day you were born, is stored in your unconscious like the archives of a supercomputer.

>>>>>>>>>>>>>>>>>>>>>>>>>>>>>>>>>>>>>>>

> Everything you have ever learnt, every memory you have ever made, every feeling you have ever felt, every habit you have ever formed, your beliefs, all your morals and values, are all hardwired in the unconscious as your survival blueprint.

>>>>>>>>>>>>>>>>>>>>>>>>>>>>>>>>>>>>>>>

If something you experienced once felt bad (unsafe), your unconscious triggers you to avoid that 'bad' experience again and triggers you to do something that makes you 'feel good' (safe).

Once programmed, you then have access to all that information on 'automatic pilot.'
The prime directive of the unconscious mind is protection and survival. It operates like the hard drive of a computer and simply accepts without prejudice what we program it to do. It does not have the capacity for analysis or logic, like your conscious thinking mind.

When you do something initially that 'comforts' you in some way (makes your unconscious recognize a 'safe' experience or a positive chemical reaction internally), it responds as if that is the cause for you being alive (surviving). It now triggers that same response as a protective mechanism. It continues to run the same programs unless you know how to update the program to install new software that says, "That habit is no longer 'safe'. Here is the new 'safe' blueprint instead."

This is not a perfect system. It works well when it works, and it takes some rewiring when it doesn't, but it's the only system we've got.

CHAPTER 2: CONSCIOUS MIND AND UNCONSCIOUS URGES AND CRAVINGS

> When a program is learned by the unconscious mind that doesn't serve us well, like anxiety, phobias, panic attacks, negative beliefs and unhelpful habits, then we need to know how to update the program and inform the unconscious that we are safe with the change.

Just like your habits are originally programmed for a positive purpose, even anxiety and phobias are designed initially to protect you. Most people just want to get 'rid' of the anxiety or phobia, it's counterintuitive to say the anxiety or phobia is a positive thing. But anxiety is the unconscious mind's way of protecting you from the thing that caused you to feel unsafe at some point in your life.

Your unconscious can even trigger anxiety if you don't do the 'habit' because, for the subconscious, the habit is what made you 'safe' in the first place.

As mentioned, once you program something into the unconscious mind, it is very difficult to change that pattern consciously. If you have a phobia, you can try to overcome it by telling yourself it's okay. Logically you know you're safe but, if the unconscious mind is running a program that's screaming 'terror', no matter what you tell yourself consciously, the unconscious mind will stay on the path of anxious action - your stress hormones are triggered, your heart pounds, your breathing changes, legs wobble, you may break out in a sweat, become dizzy, perhaps even pass out.

Anything you logically say to yourself will bounce off the unconscious fear barrier because it is your unconscious mind that is in control, doing what it has been programmed to do to keep you 'alive'.

Robert's story

Robert came to see me to overcome 'the habit' that had become his phobia to rats. A phobia he had put up with his whole life had become a problem. He was seeing rats not only in the rubbish room of his apartment block but also when he was working the night shift at Martin Place train station in Sydney, and at night the train platforms were teeming with rats!

It was affecting his work because the fear of rats was so overwhelming, he would have to ask his boss if he could go home. This acute fear of rats originated from his childhood. Robert grew up on a farm and he distinctly remembered two events that caused him to fear rats.

- Once, as he played with his friends outside, one of his friends dangled a very large dead rat in his face and
- a rat tried to crawl up his leg inside his trousers, and he had to use a stick to push it out. He remembered being terrified.

Now, as an adult, when he saw a rat, he logically knew the rat wasn't going to kill him. However, his very powerful unconscious mind tried to protect him by triggering panic as a response to the 'perceived danger'.

Once Robert had his treatment and we changed that programming in his unconscious mind, he no longer had a fear of rats.

The unconscious mind also controls our habits

The conscious part of our mind is how we begin the process of learning a new habit but, until we reinforce that as the new 'safe' blueprint to the unconscious, nothing changes permanently.

CHAPTER 2: CONSCIOUS MIND AND UNCONSCIOUS URGES AND CRAVINGS

Once we practice something often enough, we often don't make conscious decisions about it anymore. The habit becomes an unconscious process and you do the thought, action or emotional reaction automatically.

Think about the reason you chose to read this book and the behavior, or reaction, you wish to change. The impetus for the habit is located in the unconscious part of your mind. If it sometimes feels like it is out of your conscious control, then you're right.

◇◇

The impulse for the habit is in fact controlling you! It is not your fault!

◇◇

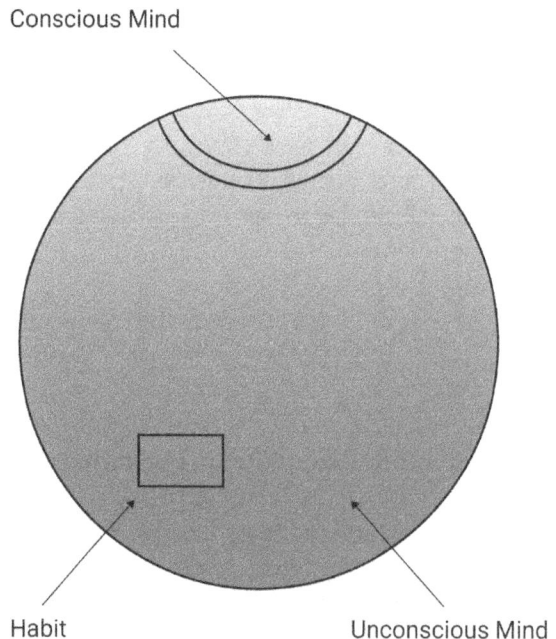

Part of the programming of the addiction to the impulse for the habit is the triggers and associations.

> **Example 1:**
>
> Imagine that a person has developed an addiction to the habit of drinking a bottle of wine every night. While visiting in-laws who don't drink alcohol, the person is perfectly fine for the week without drinking alcohol.
>
> **Example 2:**
>
> Imagine if someone has a problem with gambling. After work every day, they have an impulse to head to the betting shop. However, when on holiday to a remote island for three weeks, they don't think about the betting shop or the impulse to gamble.

In both examples, the triggers for the habit are not present. In the case of alcohol, the trigger may have been 'me-time', being at home in a quiet space to themselves, loneliness, timeout, television, or perhaps a timing trigger by preparing dinner or a reward for a good day's work. Those triggers were not present, the addiction to those habits with alcohol were no longer present either.

In the case of the gambler, the trigger might have been anticipating or actually seeing the betting shop, perhaps a reward for the end of a day at work, avoiding or delaying a troubling environment at home, loneliness and a way to connect with others, the habit of procrastination to avoid chores or confrontations, or fear of facing a troublesome challenge.

When there is a change to the environment and there are no triggers to stimulate the impulse for the habit, the unconscious triggers remain dormant until the person is back in their normal routine.

◇◇

What this tells us about habits and addictions is, in the majority of circumstances, an addiction to a habit is a psychological urge, not a biological need.

◇◇

In the next chapter, I take you through the basics of reprograming the unconscious triggers for the habits and help you understand how to take control.

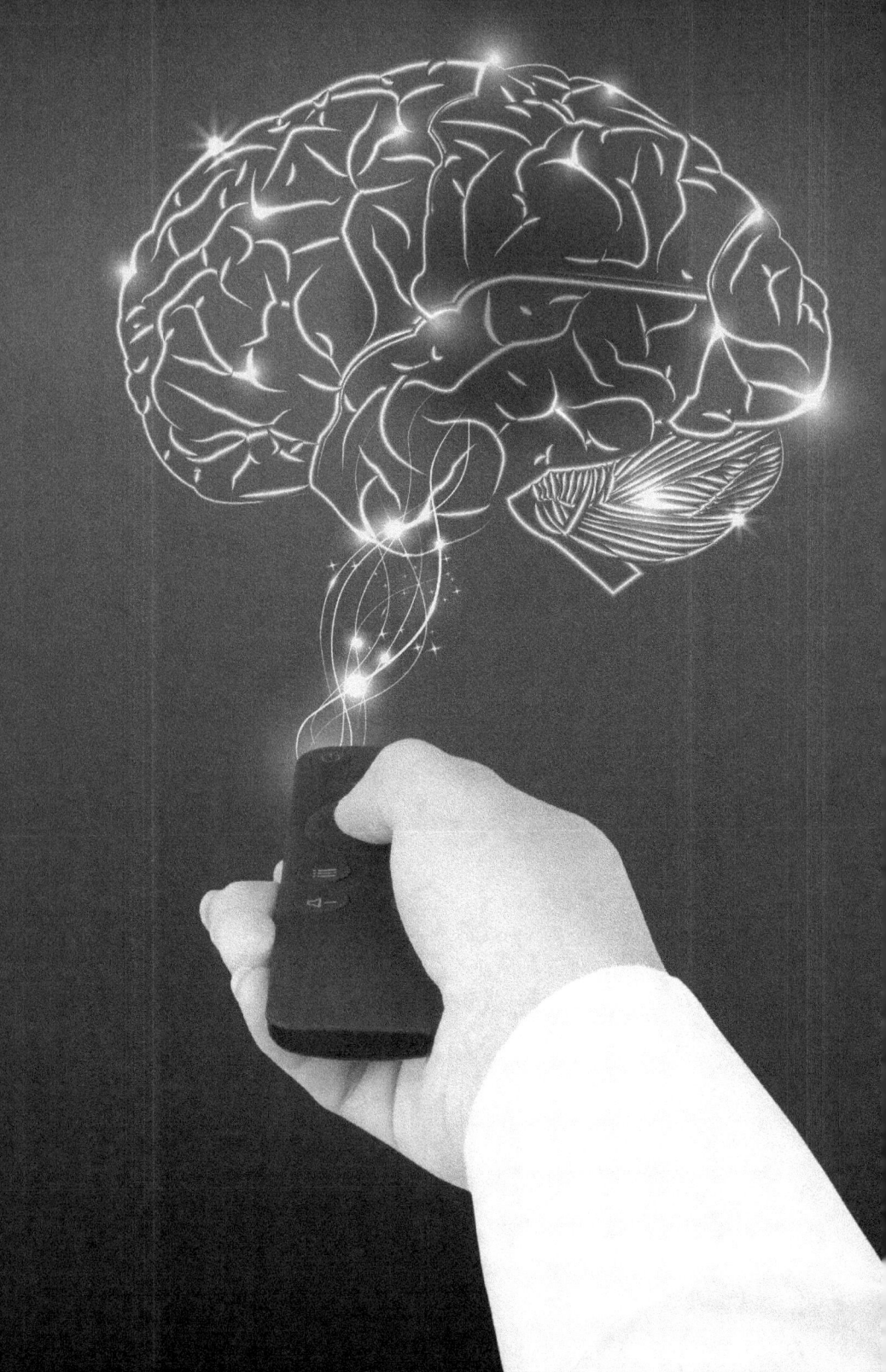

CHAPTER 3
Reprogram Your Mind to Take Control

In the previous chapters, I addressed the fact that when someone has an addiction, it is usually a deep-seated habit at the unconscious level of the mind. The behavior or thinking has occurred so often it feels as if the person has little or no control over the habit when a trigger happens.

The habit becomes an unconscious behavior, just like the phobia or panic attack example I gave earlier.

Whether our unconscious programming is considered a 'bad' habit or a 'good' habit, or a good emotion or a bad one, is determined by our current perceptions of the world and our current desired goals.

If what was once an acceptable or wanted habit has become unconscious but we now want to change this programming, how do we make that happen?

Some people can manage to change the programming through sheer willpower, with personal development and with self-help awareness.

When I was young, my eating habits were quite healthy but, in my 20s, I met my husband-to-be and took up his habit of eating chocolate and potato chips and drinking soft drinks every weekend. I programmed my unconscious with unhealthy eating habits. Luckily, I had a fast metabolism and it didn't initially affect my weight. Then I became pregnant and, after I gave birth to my first child, I found it difficult to lose the extra 65 pounds that I'd gained.

I began work as a weight-loss coach, so I had an incentive to set a good example for my clients. I began reprogramming my eating habits and was eventually able to lose the extra weight. Over the past 14 years, I have kept reprogramming my eating habits and re-triggered the healthy programming around food that I had when I was young. I have done this by eating smaller portions, avoiding sugar, drinking water and, at the same time, working on my mind by taking care of what I read and listen to.

But it's taken 15 years to trust this to be an unconscious change. I can see now, through consistency, persistence, determination and the incentive to set a good example, I have created new, improved eating habits and a better relationship with food.

In our 'microwave' and fast-food society, when so many of us juggle dozens of balls in the air, it takes an immense desire to change in order to overcome an addiction to a psychological habit by sheer willpower alone.

Imagine your teeny-weeny conscious mind that can only retain its focus on a very small amount of input (triggers beyond our conscious awareness). This tiny part of our mind can't compete with the all-powerful unconscious mind that sees, hears, feels, smells, senses and experiences EVERYTHING.

Conscious vs Unconscious Processes

It is estimated that your unconscious processes roughly 11 million pieces of information per second.

Compared to the estimate for your conscious mind which is approximately 40 bits of information per second.

11 million vs 40?

It's little wonder that our conscious willpower is often overwritten by impulses we feel we have no control over.

Instead of willpower, there is a more efficient, effective and far more powerful way to re-program your unconscious mind: clinical hypnosis or hypnotherapy.

Hypnotherapy is a very healthy, safe and natural path to retrain your unconscious with a new 'safe' comfort zone of your choice.

There are different brainwave states that range from the gamma and beta states of alertness and consciousness, to meditative and trance states of alpha and theta and the sleep states such as delta.

If your brainwaves fluctuate between the beta and theta states, then you are in various levels of a trance state. On average, a person's brainwaves enter a natural trance state seven to 10 times each day. This means everyone can enter a trance state naturally or be guided to a trance state during a hypnotherapy treatment.

Brain Wave Patterns

Gamma (<25 Hz)	Heightened perception, peaked concentration
Beta (13 - 25 Hz)	Awake and mentally alert
Alpha (8 - 12 Hz)	Relaxed state during light meditation, daydreaming, just before falling asleep or waking up
Theta (4 - 7 Hz)	Light sleep or deep meditation
Delta (1 - 3 Hz)	Deep sleep

CHAPTER 3: REPROGRAM YOUR MIND TO TAKE CONTROL

Your brainwaves naturally enter into a trance state when you are focused internally or on a particular task or experience. An example is a 'driving' trance, or a television trance while watching a show or video you become engrossed in. You may enter a trance state when reading a good book or playing a video game or when meditating.

Your brainwaves also naturally go through the trance brainwave states of Alpha and Theta when you go to sleep at night, before falling into the sleep stage. If we do this naturally, we can, therefore, assume that everybody can experience the hypnotic state.

If you can fall asleep, you can be hypnotized. If you lose track of time while reading or playing a video game, you can be hypnotized.

If you want to achieve change, learning how to self-direct a trance state, or seeking the services of a qualified hypnosis practitioner, will make your ability to achieve change far easier.

During a trance state, your brain has entered the learning and enhanced memory state. New neural connections are formed when you experience sensations and emotions, as you focus your attention on what you want to achieve while in trance.

Referring back to the 5-Step System that I introduced you to at the beginning of this book, you can be guided to work through those five steps during a hypnosis treatment or, with practice, you can learn how to guide yourself into trance and begin the process of reprogramming too.

In Chapter 4, I move you forward to begin working on the first specific habit covered in this book - the attachment to cigarettes and nicotine. Let's use the 5-Step System to quit smoking easily using the trance state to reprogram your new 'safe' attachment to being smoke free.

CHAPTER 4
Smoking – How to Quit

The majority of my Quit Smoking clients come to me believing that nicotine is addictive.

'Nicotine addiction' is often written about and talked about, but the truth is nicotine is not addictive! And this is why clients walk out of my clinic after a two-hour session as non-smokers and experience no 'withdrawal symptoms'.

Most people start smoking when they are in their teens. Even though most describe their first cigarette as making them feel sick, tasting awful and experiencing light headedness and head spins, their unconscious gained a positive emotional benefit beyond the physical reaction. As the unconscious can process millions of bits of information in a second, the positive data received by the unconscious overrides the physical rejection, and the impulse to receive that positive stimuli again is formed.

Perhaps the positive was a deep joy at feeling 'grown up' and 'independent', or a sense of 'bonding' and 'connecting' with their friends or others that they admired. Or maybe it was a sense that smoking was a 'cool' thing to do which made them feel as though they had a certain status and that, in turn, lifted their self-esteem.

Whatever the specific positive input, the unconscious received a positive 'payoff' that overrode the physical impact of the first and subsequent early cigarettes.

If a young person tried smoking but didn't feel the same unconscious 'bond', then the dislike of the cigarette in those early stages would override any impulse to repeat the experience. This person does not take up the habit of smoking.

CHAPTER 4: SMOKING – HOW TO QUIT

The Changing Perception of Smoking

[1]Until the turn of the 19th century, smoking was considered a dirty habit and was unpopular. For women, it was thought to be unladylike. If you smoked, you were deemed 'loose and immoral'.

With the development of mass-produced cigarettes that were clean and easy to use, society began to change its perception. During World War 1, soldiers' ration packs included cigarettes and they were highly valued as a way of finding comfort in a stressful environment.

By 1929, media campaigns had sold the message to men that smoking was a normal, masculine thing to do, but there was still a social taboo against women smoking.

[2] The American cigarette company, Great American Tobacco, were desperate to come up with a campaign to change this image and *hired several young women to smoke their 'torches of freedom' (Lucky Strikes) as they marched down Fifth Avenue* at the much-publicized event of the Easter Sunday parade in New York.

Other marketing methods were used to make smoking acceptable for women, including supplying and paying female Hollywood stars to give endorsements in advertisements for brands of cigarettes. Tobacco marketing also provided lessons to women on how to smoke.

By 1940, over half the young women (16-35 years) in Britain, for example, had become smokers.

---

1   Hamos, Amanda and Haglundb, Margaretha "From Social Taboo to 'torch of freedom': the marketing of cigarettes to women. BMJ Journals Vol., 9, Issue 1
2   Reeve, Michael, "Cigarette Consumption" May 2018

> Now, when I see a client for Quit Smoking, and I ask them why they think they started smoking, the two most common reasons quoted are:
>
> 1. Smoking 'looked cool'
> 2. Everybody else did it

Those two messages originated from tobacco companies' worldwide media campaigns throughout the 20th century.

Marketing messages trigger the unconscious processes with emotional messages, linking products to desired outcomes.

The reason cigarettes are believed to be difficult to quit is because there are so many emotional triggers and associations connected to them, some dating back to our childhood and the marketing messages we were exposed to. Most smokers started their habit at a young age and some of the most common triggers are:

1. First thing in the morning
2. Driving
3. After food
4. To have a break at work
5. When bored
6. When stressed
7. When drinking alcohol
8. When socializing with other smokers

When a smoker attempts to abstain from smoking but is triggered to, they experience strong cravings, which is why they assume nicotine is addictive.

CHAPTER 4: SMOKING – HOW TO QUIT

When I was in my early 20s, I worked in hospitality in both New Zealand and in the United Kingdom. In those countries at that time, it was legal to smoke inside hotels and restaurants. In fact, while working there, I inhaled cigarette smoke every day, yet I never became addicted to nicotine.

In fact, nicotine patches only have a 6% success rate to help smokers quit.

When a smoker tries to quit smoking using nicotine patches, the patch floods the body with nicotine, yet the person still wants to smoke, and they still get cravings. If the habit is as simple as a nicotine addiction, then a nicotine patch would stop the habit of smoking, wouldn't it?

The answer is no, the habit is the psychological and emotional attachment to the physical act of smoking plus the emotional bond that connected the person to the habit when they first started to smoke. Later there are also the secondary and tertiary emotional attachments made over many years of smoking.

It's also very common for smokers to miraculously stop smoking for nine months during pregnancy because their unconscious mind doesn't want to harm their unborn baby. Similarly, smokers can go on a long-haul flight without a cigarette. They don't become ill during that time; they don't need a doctor because their unconscious and conscious mind knows they can't smoke on a plane.

When smokers have a hypnotherapy treatment and that deep-seated habit is broken, they walk out feeling like a non-smoker, even though the nicotine is still in their body for the next one to three days.

The three main reasons clients give me for wanting to quit are:

1. Health
2. Family
3. Cost

The treatment I use for clients to become a non-smoker is very powerful. Studies prove it has a 97% success rate. You too can follow the 5-Step System. That's 6% using patches or 97% success when you use my system.

THE 5-STEP SYSTEM

Step 1: Discovery

Discover the habits and associations related to having a cigarette. Be curious about common triggers and find out the reason the client wants to quit, what they dislike about smoking and what they are looking forward to gaining when they become a non-smoker. Discover what their family history is and their current environment to decipher whether they are in an environment that will support them to quit.

Ask lots of questions:

- How long have they been a smoker?
- Are they consciously aware of why they started?
- Have they tried to quit? If so, what methods have they tried?
- An important part of this step is to ensure that the client actually wants to stop smoking. If they want to quit, the

treatment should be effective. If they don't want to quit, then the treatment probably won't work because no hypnotherapist can *make* a client do something they don't want to do.

As a hypnotherapist, I can take away the cravings, break the habit and disconnect the triggers but I can't take away a client's free will.

Step 2: Decision Point

It is very rare for smoking to be a symptom of a deeper trauma. Even my clients who suffer from anxiety, panic attacks, depression or PTSD usually have no problem breaking the habit of smoking through hypnosis.

I've even had clients who have suffered from anxiety directly before and even after their treatment, and their history and relationship with anxiety has not affected their result to stop smoking.

On the very rare occasion that a client hasn't quit after a second session, I would treat secondary and tertiary gains and test for a deeper trauma underlying the smoking. Once I have treated the trauma, I would then go back to treat the smoking to break the habit for good.

Step 3: Expectations During and After Treatment

Sometimes when clients see me, they joke that they don't want to cluck like a chicken. I'll take the time to explain that hypnotherapy is different to a hypnosis stage show where audience members are called up on the stage to do various spectacles, such as pretending to be a chicken. Only a small percentage of the population can be hypnotized quickly and easily for a stage show, and these are the people that the hypnotist will pre-select. People who tend to volunteer to be on stage for a hypnosis show are one of three types:

1. Curious
2. Skeptical
3. Extroverted, someone who is comfortable being the center of attention.

Each person on stage is still in control the entire time and, if the hypnotist were to push them beyond what they would normally be comfortable doing, they would immediately come out of hypnosis. If you've ever seen a stage show, the number of volunteers gradually diminish as they are pushed to their limits. The hypnotist is normally left with only a few people by the end of the show who are still in trance responding to what is asked of them.

That's why during those shows you will see the hypnotist telling people they can leave the stage and go back to their seats as they become more aware of their surrounding and stop responding to the suggestions.

Those who are left are usually the susceptible and the extroverts. Both will do what is asked and entertain the crowd. The hypnotist was searching for those few within the initial volunteer group.

However, with clinical hypnotherapy, everyone can reach the stage of trance that enables the brain to learn. You do not need to be highly susceptible like the volunteers the stage hypnotist is looking for. A hypnotherapist only needs to educate the client on what hypnotherapy is and what it will feel like and help them understand that it's the kind of hypnosis that allows their brain to help them achieve their goals and that they already experience it every day when they daydream or lose track of time while they're focused intently on something.

Therefore, everybody can be hypnotized to the level needed to access therapeutic change.

The state the therapist is helping you to achieve is simply like the gentle feeling before you doze off into a peaceful sleep. But it's not the sleep you would normally experience at night; this is a daydream-like sleep when you often realize you are aware but are unaware of time and space. You drift in and out of conscious awareness, often aware of what the therapist is saying and sometimes drifting off and wondering what they just said.

It's a timeless experience, just like when you lose track of time when reading a good book or watching a movie.

Can a person resist the treatment?

Yes, a person can be resistant to hypnosis during their treatment. Personally, I have experienced it only twice while working with thousands of clients. It can be resolved by addressing how the client is feeling, helping them release whatever is holding them back and making sure they feel safe and comfortable with the session and the therapist.

What it does or doesn't feel like

I tell my clients not to expect to 'feel hypnotized' or 'under' hypnosis. I inform them to just expect to feel more relaxed and be curious that the length of time will seem either shorter or longer than they expect.

Everyone experiences hypnosis in their own way, and that can range from a state of full awareness to a state of deep relaxation. I assure my clients that they will be aware of what is happening, but they might just lose track of time. Most of my clients tend to think a session went a lot quicker than it actually did, but it does not affect a client's results if they were in a lighter trance and felt fully aware. Sometimes I'll have a client who has a concern that I'll be telling them what to do and, in their words, they are "strong minded" or "don't like being told what to do". However, hypnosis is not something that is *done to you*; it is a process that you are guided through and you are always in control and can accept or resist any suggestion. Despite what popular television shows try to portray, you cannot be hypnotized against your will. If a suggestion is outside your conscience, values or morals, you simply bring yourself to full awareness because you were always in control to decide what to accept.

Step 4: Treatment

The treatment is usually one hypnotherapy session, after which most clients regain control and feel like a non-smoker. The approach I use is specifically tailored for the individual client. Whatever information they have shared with me, I'll use in their treatment. Everything that we discussed in Step 1 is added to the session: the client's triggers, what they dislike about smoking, the benefits they look forward to as a non-smoker and how their life will look as a non-smoker. Often a client will feel nervous when they arrive, usually because of their fear of failure, but sometimes it's because they have little understanding of what we will be doing throughout the treatment. However, by the end of the treatment, they feel confident, relaxed and very happy.

If a client feels as if they're struggling after their treatment, it means that a part of their unconscious still thinks that smoking is good for them. This is called a secondary or tertiary gain. This can happen to clients who consciously despise smoking yet some part of them is still attached to the cigarettes or an aspect of the habit. Struggling can come in many forms: negative emotions or cravings. This can be easily resolved with a second treatment by working with 'that part' of the unconscious mind to clear the unconscious attachment.

Step 5: Post-Treatment

It is very important that a client is informed as to how to support themselves to remain a non-smoker after their treatment.

The biggest difference they will notice is that they feel in control. When the old triggers arise, such as a coffee or a friend who offers them a cigarette, they can remember they don't need or want to smoke. It's a completely different mindset.

It's normal in the first week or two to have thoughts about smoking, the occasional flash of the thought of a cigarette that passes through their mind, but often the immediate thought straight after is, "I don't smoke."

For those days immediately after the session, the therapy is still processing and that desire not to smoke becomes stronger every day. For some clients, it may even be a little bit like a rollercoaster, but it's very important in these early days for them not to have a cigarette because it will trigger the unconscious to activate the old neural pathways (the wiring in the brain that used to trigger the urges and habit).

CASE STUDY - Natalia

Natalia remembers having direct access to cigarettes at the age of 10. Her mother used to smoke, so she used to ask Natalia to go to the shops and buy her cigarettes. Her first cigarette was with her friends at 11. It seemed cool to hang with friends and smoke back then. By the age of 16, she considered herself a full-time smoker.

By the time she was 19, Natalia had tried to quit smoking cold turkey. She succeeded for six months but relapsed one night when she went out for a few drinks with friends. For the next 10 years, Natalia surrendered and enjoyed smoking. By the time she was 29, she realized she had to stop. Now she was in a new relationship and her partner was anti-smoking.

In the past, Natalia enjoyed running and swimming. She loved being fit but the motivation to keep it up was harder to come by. Even living by the beach with plenty of opportunities didn't help.

Natalia realized that her energy and health were affected, smoking was costing a small fortune and she hated seeing her hard-earned money wasted. It was then the real battle started!

She tried cold turkey again then moved to nicotine patches, nicotine lozenges and e-cigarettes, but all methods failed. Natalia became more frustrated and disappointed. The struggle went on for another two years until she booked in with us for her treatment on the 11th of November 2017. She has been a non-smoker ever since!

She was amazed that it had been so easy to stop in the end. After the treatment, Natalia felt relaxed and the cravings were gone. She did try to have a cigarette once but felt sick, her throat became sore, she got a headache and she vomited.

Natalia has found that everything is better as a non-smoker. She has noticed that her body, mind and relationships have all changed for the better. Happier and healthier now, when she is out with friends who still smoke, she has no desire to join in at all.

Her advice for those who are thinking of stopping is, "Do not give up, the treatment has worked for me, and it will work for you. Don't wait any longer. Life is better without cigarettes!"

If you need help to stop smoking, please reach out to me at www.activatehypnotherapy.com.au or to download a free hypnosis audio to release the 'strangler fig' of habits and addictions go to www.isitahabitoranaddiction.com/resources

In Chapter 5, it's time to address a very different habit - the one we have with food. The differences between food and smoking are quite significant because, when we stop smoking, we can live without cigarettes. However, when we address a poor relationship with food, we still need to eat. We cannot live for long without food.

CHAPTER 5

Food - How to Have a Healthy Relationship

The world is experiencing an obesity epidemic. According to worldpopulationreview.com, in 2019, the number of obese people in the world was approximately 2.1 billion, which made up about 30% of the total population. This number continues to rise. Over 3 million people die from obesity-related illness each year. The worldwide obesity rate has tripled since 1975.

A few years ago, I attended a lecture from Dr Gary Small, MD, Director of the Geriatric Psychiatry Division at the Semel Institute for Neuroscience and Human Behavior. Dr. Small revealed obesity statistics showing the obesity rate was decreasing substantially for those who were over the age of 50.

He asked the audience why there was a lower obesity rate for people over the age of 50 and the answer was that the obese people began to die once they reached 50.

The number one cause of death around the world is diet related. Eating the wrong foods and overeating all kinds of food can cause issues such as diabetes, heart disease, cancer and stroke.

Food in the Western world has become associated with pleasure, socializing and emotional stressors. We celebrate special occasions with food. We catch up with friends over breakfast, brunch, lunch and dinner. We invite people over for parties with food, movies with snacks, and drinks with nibbles. We barbecue, we picnic, we bake, sauté and grill.

CHAPTER 5: FOOD - HOW TO HAVE A HEALTHY RELATIONSHIP

Food has become the focus of our happiness, sadness, grief and hurt.

If we feel depressed, we reach for chocolate or our favorite cookie or snack.

During the 1890s, a Russian physiologist called Ivan Pavlov in his research predicted that dogs would salivate when food was placed in front of them. What he noted however, was that the dogs actually began to salivate as soon as they heard the footsteps of his assistant bringing the food.

Through further studies, which have since became famous, the dogs were conditioned to salivate at the sound of a bell.

And that's exactly what the big fast food chains do by using clever marketing campaigns! Your brain learns with emotional or sensory stimulus. Marketing is based on emotional purchasing habits, and your brain likes the emotional messages used by big brands.

Visual and Auditory Triggers

People who like Coca Cola, or big brand soda drinks, see an advertisement with the logo for their favorite brand and suddenly have the urge and want one, in the same way that the dogs in Pavlov's study suddenly salivated at the sound of a bell. Seeing the logo, or hearing the jingle, triggers your brain, your taste buds and your salivary glands – your memory is activated to fantasize about the taste, the cold and the fizzy sensation, and you want to reach for one.

> *We know that fast food is fattening and too much causes weight gain, yet the queue for McDonald's and other fast food brands are always the longest, while the queue for the salad bar is often the shortest.*

Brands like McDonald's provide a consistent experience every time: employees recite a scripted greeting, the menu looks the same, and the same images and logos are posted on the walls. The more consistent the experience, the more your brain associates even the colors of the brand with being hungry and the expectation of the 'same' experience each time.

At the time of writing this book, I am working with a Virtual Gastric Band Hypnosis client. She mentioned recently that, since chatting to me about the programming of the unconscious, it has made her more aware and she has noticed that every time her three-year-old son sits down to watch television, he automatically asks for food, even if he has just eaten a meal. The association has been made and will continue until someone more conscious of the links chooses to do something about that link.

More than ever before, the Western population is suffering from addictions to the habit of eating sugar and junk food.

Like generations of children growing up in Western society, I grew up listening to my grandparents lecturing me about the starving children in Africa and how it was important to eat everything on my plate (even if I wasn't hungry).

My grandfather couldn't help but serve me huge portions at mealtimes because it was all he had ever known but, in the 1920s, when he was a child, food choices were limited, and people were more active.

As I mentioned in Chapter 3, it's very difficult to change a lifetime of habits through working with the conscious mind only. Luckily for me, despite the lectures, I got away with eating very little and running back outside to play.

With the 5-Step System, you'll be able to disconnect triggers to stress, learn to love and drink enough water, feel fuller faster, increase your metabolism, reject sugar and junk food, even to the point of switching off the urges and impulses for them.

CASE STUDY - Carl

Carl had always loved food. He'd also had a sweet tooth his whole life, and particularly loved eating ice cream and cake. His active lifestyle meant he stayed in a healthy weight range, but it also meant he didn't have time to eat regularly.

That all changed in 2013 when he contracted the debilitating tropical disease of Ross River Fever. His energy levels were affected, and he began to put on weight. He not only was sick with the virus and had no energy but also now had no motivation.

Carl craved sweets even more, and back then he didn't realize sugar was making the aches and pains worse and aggravating his arthritis. Carl was confined to the house, feeling bored and depressed. He 'felt' hungry and grazed on food all day and his weight spiraled out of control. He would eat sweets, bread, sugary buns, and oftentimes even the kids' after-school treats as well before they got home from school.

Despite eating all day, he then ate a large evening meal, followed by snack foods all evening. He was also drinking two energy drinks per day. In Carl's words, "I became a human vacuum cleaner!" Within 12 months, Carl weighed 113 kilos.

Carl had no willpower. He knew what he should do to lose the extra weight, but he couldn't stop doing the opposite.

That all changed when he booked in for his treatment in 2018. After the first session, he noticed that he suddenly had willpower and felt more in control. It was Easter and people were eating and offering him Easter eggs. However, he found that he had control and was able to rationalize that sugar would cause him to feel hungry again and he didn't actually want the chocolate eggs anyway. After one treatment, he had transformed from a human vacuum cleaner to only wanting to eat three small, regular meals per day.

At the time of writing this book, Carl has maintained a weight of 90kgs for over a year. His relationship with food has completely changed since his treatment. He no longer desires junk food, sweet treats or soft drinks. He eats small portion sizes at mealtimes because he feels more satisfied on far less food.

Carl has more energy and vitality and feels healthier. He laughs proudly that, "This is the best shape I have been in since I was 18 years old."

CHAPTER 5: FOOD - HOW TO HAVE A HEALTHY RELATIONSHIP

FOOD ADDICTION EXPERT – Josette Freeman

Josette Freeman is the senior national program coordinator at SMART Recovery (Self-Management and Recovery Training), a non-profit organization since 2007 that originated in America. Her role is to train facilitators around Australia and New Zealand to run SMART Recovery groups for those with unhealthy relationships with food and other addictions as well. There are now over 350 groups throughout Australia and New Zealand.

Josette shares a story about a woman who attended the program to help with her food addiction. She didn't look overweight, but she felt that she was. The other people in the group couldn't understand why she was there but, by the end of the program, they were embracing her because she had been doing exactly the same thing as people do when they gamble, drink or take drugs. She lied about her food, she hid her food and her self-esteem plummeted the more she did it. Her behavior was exactly the same as everybody else's in the group.

Usually clients who attend the meetings for food addictions are comfort eating. They are overeating on highly sugared carbohydrates. SMART Recovery focuses on improving self-esteem and asking 'why' constant eating happens, what triggers it, and is it a coping strategy? Are there better coping strategies that you can put in place rather than eating?

SMART Recovery is a program for clients to learn how to develop self-management skills. It's not a therapy or counseling session. The facilitators are trauma-informed but it's not a forum to unpack trauma. Instead, if trauma does come into the equation, the facilitators will put it back onto the client by asking them how they can get further help.

Josette believes that food addiction can be both a habit created and caused by an underlying trauma.

Josette believes that food addiction can be both a habit created *and* caused by an underlying trauma. It starts with a person enjoying food. The food gives them comfort and it feels good, so they eat more. By the time they realize it has become problematic, it's gone too far to consciously pull back straight away. The ambivalence comes from thinking that it's not really that bad, or that life is really bad at the moment, so they'll leave dealing with the food intake because there is so much other chaos going on around them.

Other problems can develop, such as health issues like diabetes or high blood pressure, congested skin or bad teeth, or there is frustration at not finding clothes to fit or a loss of confidence and self-esteem. Women, in particular, feel pressure, from themselves and from society, to be slim. All of this leads to their becoming more and more unhappy.

One of the features of the SMART Recovery program is having a plan for the next seven days. The program only concentrates on the last seven days and the next seven days. The plan for the next seven days might be to delay eating food every time they get upset or to not go down aisle 12 at the supermarket because that's where the chocolates are.

The program focuses on coping with urges and problem solving - for example, switching to a glass of water and cutting up a piece of fruit to eat when watching television rather than eating crisps, cookies or chocolate or writing a shopping list before going to the supermarket and buying only what's on the list and then leaving.

CHAPTER 5: FOOD - HOW TO HAVE A HEALTHY RELATIONSHIP

And then there's the lifestyle balance that can get out of whack. If you have been spending a lot of time eating, then you will need to come up with a plan to fill that time with other non-food related meaningful activities.

If you have been spending a lot of time eating, then you will need to come up with a plan to fill that time with other non-food related meaningful activities.

Clients can attend up to two or three groups per week. One key point reiterated during group time is to practice whatever is being learnt in the group. There is no point saying, "Tick, I've been to a group," and then going home and not using the tools provided. The participants in the group set the agenda for the session rather than the facilitator. And it's a mutual aid group - they help one another. They're taught the process of how to help one another.

The facilitator is not there to provide the answers or solve the problem. For example, a participant might say, "I had a terrible fight with my mother and went straight for the chocolate." Rather than the facilitator saying, "How about not having chocolate in the house?" the facilitator would ask them, "What could you do other than eating the chocolate?" and allow the participant to come up with their own strategy.

The strategies are all going to be the same: delay, distract and keep busy doing something else.

Clients start off at different levels of motivation and the program works through four different target points of building and maintaining motivation. Most clients come in fairly ambivalent about making a change and, as they work through the program, they realize it's easier and more helpful than they thought.

SMART Recovery is not an abstinence-based group. They are working within a 'harm minimization' framework.

Success is not viewed by how many people stop the unhelpful eating behavior but by changing their thinking about themselves and food. If someone says, "I haven't had any cookies this week," there's no way of knowing whether this is truly the case - the other members of the group are not with them at home to see if there is a change. But, when someone begins to interact in the group and challenges their own thinking and other people's thinking, then the facilitator can see the improvement and change. That is considered the success.

Past studies conducted by SMART Recovery have shown clearly its participants have improved mental health and wellbeing from attending the program.

To put it in simple terms, SMART Recovery teaches people how to manage uncomfortable feelings. As when taking drugs, gambling or drinking alcohol, people eat when they are not feeling comfortable. SMART Recovery is all about helping people to become 'unstuck' and to support them to move on rather than to stay in the present or the past. And, once they have the tools to do that, things improve rapidly for them.

SMART Recovery focuses on people's behaviors, their thinking, and challenging their beliefs. It's an approach that is very practical and solution-focused.

The process to overcome binge eating or emotional eating

Josette says, "Number one is getting the client talking about what it is that they want to say about binge eating. What do they want to talk about or focus on?"

Because binge eating is a huge topic, the specific aspect for the client has to be narrowed down.

A client might mention that, as soon as they come home from work, they go straight to the refrigerator. So, now there's a specific pattern to focus on - that little time period where they can do one thing differently to change that pattern.

Josette continues, "You can help the client come up with an alternative thing to do before they even walk in the door, or by entering the house by a different door and going straight to a different part of the house to do something else first thing."

Over time, as the discussion continues, it can expand naturally to why they think they need to go straight to the fridge.

"It might be that they find their job very stressful," Josette says, "and going to the fridge to find a snack first thing becomes the 'outlet' to reward or numb out the day. So, then you'd go back to address the stress of work and finding ways to manage work challenges differently so they're not coming home and binge eating. "

The discussion is client-led and solution-focused. SMART Recovery doesn't focus on the 'story', it focuses on the solutions; the small steps that mean the client can change one small thing at a time.

"With other addictions, you can break the habit and be free of that substance or habit for life. But, with food addiction, you still have to eat for survival." Juanita Smith

---

So, by necessity, you have to break the habit whilst eating every day and at the same time you must also reprogram the unconscious mind to choose the right foods in the right quantity. Working with clients for food addiction can be quite a process. That's where the 5-Step System comes in.

Step 1: Discovery

Discover the personal history - their specific patterns and habits with food and eating.

- What were their eating habits as they grew up?
- What sort of childhood did they have?
- Did, or do, they suffer from trauma, depression, anxiety? Usually the motivating factor to change their eating patterns and habits is to lose weight.
- What are their current habits with food that keep them overweight? Why do they want to lose the weight?
- Or, if they don't need to lose weight, what are their goals in changing their eating habits? Perhaps it's good health and more energy or related to a condition such as diabetes.
- What's their 'big why' for wanting to stop the addiction?
- How would they like to see themselves in six and 12 months?
- Do they have a special event coming up or any other goal?

What are the negatives to overeating and compulsive eating?

Step 2: Decision Point

Help the client understand the food habit they've developed is just that, a habit, not an addiction. Often, food addictions are a symptom of a deeper trauma. It is at this point that we decide if we need to work with the trauma first. If they are also looking for a weight loss solution, it is important to consider that they might be holding onto weight to keep them safe. During this step, we specifically tailor the treatment for the individual.

Step 3: Expectations During and After Treatment

It's important that the person has a realistic view of the outcomes and the expected weight loss. The challenge at first is, when they leave the clinic, the weight is still going to be there, plus they still have to eat, so it's very important that they have a few skills to help them make the right choices.

If they support themselves consciously, then the change will gradually take place at an unconscious level. The treatment is not a 'magic wand'. They have to want to change their relationship with food and give themselves ongoing support.

If the client were to work with a Personal Trainer, they would have to get up and show up every day. Or, if the client were to have Gastric Band surgery, their doctor would lay out the rules of what they could and couldn't do before and after the procedure. Similarly, the client would need to support themselves and do their part during and after the treatment and follow the guidelines laid out for best results.

Step 4: Treatment

Treatment will vary from client to client. Some clients may only have a sugar addiction attachment and not have underlying trauma to clear. Treatment would be a Neuro Linguistic Programming process followed by a hypnotherapy session.

If the excess weight and the eating stems from trauma, then hypnotherapy sessions for trauma need to be done first.

It's possible that, as a result of working with the trauma, the food addiction may disappear straightaway. However, further hypnotherapy sessions to break the addiction to food would usually need to follow.

Most often, however, there is no trauma and a program is specifically tailored for the client that includes up to four sessions.

There are many elements to cover: portion control (which is reprogrammed through hypnosis by telling the unconscious mind that the stomach is the size of a golf ball, and this is often done with the Virtual Gastric Band Hypnosis program.) This technique reminds the unconscious to drink more water, that motivation to exercise or move the body appropriately is easy, addressing general motivation, the sugar addiction, breaking the junk food addiction, and disconnecting emotional attachment to food or eating.

Step 5: Post-Treatment

It takes time for the sessions to process and there are usually many layers and secondary and tertiary gains, so, as it was mentioned to the client in Step 3 when managing their expectations, it's important that the client does their part in the days after treatment.

It's important that the client follows the post-session support instructions the therapist has laid out for them. Steps such as listening to recordings daily, utilizing a multitude of the latest mind management techniques and stress reduction strategies, are a very important part of our work together. It is absolutely essential that the client listens to the follow-up recordings at least

CHAPTER 5: FOOD - HOW TO HAVE A HEALTHY RELATIONSHIP

once per day. These will create new neural pathways in the client's brain relating to their associations and attitudes towards food. Listening to them will also reinforce the hypnotherapy sessions, helping the client to consciously make the right choices when choosing to eat.

The client is to ask themselves, "Will this serve me or hurt me? The burger and fries or the healthy salad?"

"With food, I want to finish by underlining that it takes a strong 'why' to create the strength to overcome an unhelpful relationship. But, with practice and persistence, all change is possible." Juanita Smith

In Chapter 6, I delve deep into alcohol, not the beverage itself but the habits around alcohol. The rates for enquiries to reduce alcohol have almost doubled in recent years. It is more common than you might think, and very common with women who overindulge in an extra bevy or two, and just as easy to overcome.

CHAPTER 6

Alcohol – When and How to Stop or Reduce

Like food, alcohol is a big part of our culture in the Western world. To celebrate, we pop open a bottle of champagne, drink wine to complement a meal, have a few beers when we watch sport, and a party or a barbecue isn't complete without alcohol and nibbles. We celebrate our children's coming of age, our births, deaths and marriages, our commiserations and our achievements, all with alcohol.

These triggers and associations are programmed into our unconscious mind, making alcohol consumption not only widely acceptable in our culture but also normal. Our close relationship with alcohol is present in most societies throughout history. The choice of preferred alcoholic beverages varies with each country, but the relationship has created a worldwide drinking culture.

As I mentioned previously, alcohol was a big part of my life through my teenage years and into my 20s. For many of us who experienced those teenage and early 20s binges, life goes on and, at some point, alcohol is no longer the reason for life. It settles into a place in our life that we are happy with. But for some people drinking alcohol becomes a more deep-seated habit that negatively impacts their lives for years, and sometimes decades, to come.

Stressed out mothers might get into a habit of having a glass or two of wine every day as they begin to prepare the evening meal then, before they know it, it's turned into three or four glasses a few times per week, and then an unconscious pull to have that

CHAPTER 6: ALCOHOL – WHEN AND HOW TO STOP OR REDUCE

bottle of wine or six-pack of beer, or more, every day. I frequently see both men and women in my clinic whose relationship with alcohol has become a strain on their lives and their happiness.

Eventually, if left unchecked, this can create the habit of not knowing when 'enough is enough' - no longer recognizing the time to switch on the off button. I hear stories of regret for what people have been told they've said or done, or for how they feel the next day.

if left unchecked, this can create the habit of not knowing when 'enough is enough' - no longer recognizing the time to switch on the off button.

But the key is that, at some point, alcohol dulled the senses so much they no longer had control of the ability to stop drinking until it had 'gone too far again'.

When alcohol becomes a problem, not only does it affect our ability to know when to stop, the long-term effects can cause weight gain, low energy, memory loss, a change in personality, paranoia, depression, careless behavior, lack of motivation and mood swings.

Alcohol can cause physical health challenges like stomach ulcers, acid reflux, heartburn, gastritis, heart disease, cancer, and diminished grey and white matter in the brain

Julian Docherty – Drug and Alcohol Rehabilitation Expert

Julian Docherty from The Salvation Army's Pathways Maroubra, works with drug and alcohol clients in an out-client capacity. He assists patients overcome addiction. His job is to help clients navigate the drug and alcohol sector and formulate a plan to overcome their addiction. He also facilitates groups and assessments for day programs.

Easy Access

According to Julian, alcohol addiction is a huge problem because it's easily accessible. "You can purchase it cheaply in any neighborhood, on nearly every street corner," he says.

It's also socially acceptable to have a couple of glasses of alcohol with dinner. But, with many of the clients that I see in my clinic, and the ones that Julian sees, the relationship with alcohol has usually moved way past that point.

Julian continues, "They have started to drink by themselves, they are often hiding bottles at home and are seeking help because they can see it's become a problem. Quite often, they may have some success at quitting, but they don't change the environment that triggers them in the first place, so they relapse."

Quite often, they may have some success at quitting, but they don't change the environment that triggers them in the first place, so they relapse."

I agree entirely with Julian. The triggers might be the people they hang out with, walking past the same shop that sells alcohol every day or going through stress at home or at work.

Julian adds, "People seek help at Pathways because they get to the stage where they can't get through a day without having a drink. They begin to suffer from delirium tremens (the DTs) when they stop drinking."

Delirium tremens symptoms range in severity but can include:

1. Delirium (sudden confusion)
2. Change to mental function
3. Most commonly, tremors
4. Quite often agitation and irritability
5. Overexcitement or anxiety and fear
6. Hallucinations
7. Extreme and long sleep (over a day or longer)

Further signs that the relationship with alcohol needs attention are when people get to the point that they are drinking large quantities - usually two or three liters, if not more.

When a person drinks that quantity, it affects the body, they don't eat, and, most often, a bout of vomiting ensues.

> This stage is very dangerous because, if you try to restrict or deny yourself alcohol suddenly, you're at high risk of having a seizure. Also, a client can suffer from Korsakoff, which is more commonly referred to as 'wet brain'. This literally means your brain is swimming in fluid. Alcoholic wet brain is fatal in up to 20% of cases. This level of alcohol consumption can also cause liver damage.

Julian Docherty continues, "Sometimes clients will be drinking smaller amounts - for example, a bottle of wine. This, of course, is easier to deal with. We can put together a program with activities to distract them from drinking, such as drawing, painting, walking on the beach or joining a group. Quite often, if a person is drinking that amount, they are sitting at home by themselves, so it's a matter of helping them create a plan to keep themselves busy as the habit is reforming, getting them out and about with other people in environments where there is no alcohol involved.

"When clients first come to Pathways, the first step is to find out what their needs are and, if we can, to get their needs met.

- Firstly, find out why they are drinking
- A 12-week program is then tailored for the individual client by attending Pathways' many psychoeducational group sessions. These group sessions include a positive lifestyle program and address assertiveness, conflict resolutions, grief, resentments, anger and the 'child within.' "

Even though alcohol addiction is often trauma based, Pathways addresses this by asking the question, *"How does what happened then affect you now?"*, rather than bringing up the trauma which could retraumatize the client causing them to drink again.

It's important to remember that, once they leave somewhere like Pathways or a clinical environment, they may often be going back into a high-risk environment. In the case of Pathways, some clients choose to move on to the Salvation Army's residential rehabilitation program so they can detox and be immersed in an environment where they can dig deep and work on the trauma with a psychologist.

Julian believes that the craving for alcohol comes from a deeply ingrained habit so, to effectively break free, a person needs to:

1. Change behaviors
2. Change their social circle

3. Avoid situations where alcohol is involved
4. Start doing different activities to keep themselves busy
5. Attend SMART Recovery or AA meetings and build a good support network around themselves
6. Set goals (asking what you want from life and plan the steps for small achievable goals first)

They also need to keep doing these steps every day until a new habit is created.

CASE STUDY - Leonie

Leonie has a fulfilling but extremely busy life. When she is not running her hectic business, she and her husband love to travel and spend time with their children and grandchildren.

Leonie got into a habit of coming home from work and pouring two glasses of white wine while dinner was cooking and then finishing the bottle while eating. On her days off, or when away on holiday, there would be lots of eating out accompanied by white wine.

Pretty soon, Leonie realized that she had created a habit of drinking a bottle of white wine every day. On the rare occasion when she would drink red wine or champagne, she found that she drank a lot less and she had a stop button.

After her treatment, she stopped drinking white wine instantly and has had no desire or cravings since. If she feels like an alcoholic drink at the end of the day, or when she is eating out, she will usually have a red wine or sometimes a champagne, but she is in complete control and drinks a lot less than when she was drinking white wine.

CASE STUDY - Mary

Mary came to me to quit alcohol. She had got to the point where she was drinking one or two bottles of wine every day. It was affecting her life because she couldn't drive to pick up her kids from school – she had to walk. She wasn't getting tasks done at home because she lacked motivation. She had put on weight and, as a result, was feeling uncomfortable and less confident. She noticed that she no longer took pride in her appearance and she avoided public places because of this. She was hiding bottles around the house so her husband wouldn't notice how much she was drinking.

Mary's drinking patterns, such as drinking when the kids were at school, and the fact that the drinking was impacting her life so negatively, were warning bells that the drinking was a symptom of underlying trauma.

During the first step of her treatment – Discovery – Mary shared with me that her mother put her up for adoption when she was a baby because she was too young to care for a baby. When Mary was four years old and living with her adoptive parents, she was playing with her younger brother on the street in front of her house. He was hit by a car and killed in front of her. This caused a breakdown in her adoptive parents' marriage and they gave Mary away to relatives. Mary then suffered sexual abuse at the hands of one of their sons.

Mary's treatment consisted of four hypnotherapy sessions working on her past trauma, and a fifth session where we worked on breaking the remaining habit of drinking wine. After the first hypnotherapy session, Mary noticed a positive shift in feeling better within herself. By her fourth session, she felt lighter, more loving towards her children, more confident, happier and her anxiety had gone.

The fourth session was about programming relaxation, peacefulness and calm into her unconscious mind. By this time, she had completely cut out drinking during the day and felt that she was only having a drink in the evening out of habit. In the fifth and final hypnotherapy session, we were able to break that habit so that she now only has a rare drink on a very special occasion.

Like Leonie, many people have mistaken 'an addiction to the habit' of drinking alcohol for an addiction to alcohol. This addiction is one that can be easily broken with my 5-Step System. In Mary's case, I am also treating an addiction to the habit, however, for Mary, drinking alcohol was a symptom of underlying trauma that needed to be healed first.

Step 1: Discovery

- Learn about the client and how the habit of drinking alcohol came about.
- What were the effects of drinking alcohol?
- Why did they want to quit alcohol or cut back?

Once we have all the necessary information about the client, we can move onto Step 2.

Step 2: Decision Point

- We make a decision as to whether it is an addiction to the habit or a side effect of a deeper trauma.
- If it's an addiction to the habit, we can move onto Step 3 but, if there is an underlying trauma, then we need to treat the trauma first.

Step 3: Expectations During and After Treatment

- When we help the client manage expectations, they can support themselves and know what to expect.

Step 4: Treatment

- Work directly with the unconscious mind to break that habit,
- Disconnect any triggers and associations,
- Reprogram a new reality where the client is free and in control.

Step 5: Post-Treatment Support

- The client will feel free and in control but needs to support themselves and choose not to drink again. This will be easy, though, because their unconscious mind has been reprogrammed. We can take away the habit, disconnect the triggers and make it easy to be alcohol free, but we cannot take away a person's free will. If they choose to drink again, it is likely they will open up the old neural pathways and bring back the habit.
- If they find they are struggling at all in the future, it will be because of one of two reasons. First, they have CHOSEN to drink and have reactivated the old neural pathways and second, an event has occurred in life that is causing anxiety, stress or another negative emotion. We are only a phone call away for further treatment and to get back on track.

To summarize, alcohol is a huge part of our culture and is socially acceptable. For most people, it's something that is within their control but for others it can become an addiction stemming from a habit. Like other habits, it becomes deeply ingrained in our powerful unconscious mind and becomes automatic, thus out of our conscious control. The unconscious mind is rigid so, once it is programmed, it is difficult to change.

With my treatment I am working directly with the unconscious mind to break the unwanted habit. Sometimes there is trauma that needs to be dealt with first. That judgement is made from certain patterns and emotions with alcohol that the client is experiencing. Whether working with trauma or without trauma, once the programming has been changed on an unconscious level, the client will find they are in control and free. The client is aware that they need to support themselves into the future, but that is easy to do as long as they want to be free from alcohol. –
Juanita Smith

In the following chapter, I have addressed one of the emerging addictions to a habit that is taking Australia and many parts of the world by storm. Gambling. Whether it's a punt on a racehorse or 'a few dollars' in a slot or poker machine, gambling has become a household phenomenon.

CHAPTER 7

Gambling – How to Take Back Control

Alice Ivers – 'Poker Alice'

Alice Ivers was born in 1851 in Devonshire, England. When she was still a young girl, her father, a schoolmaster, moved the family to Virginia, United States, where Alice attended an elite boarding school for young women.

Alice met her husband, Frank Duffield, a mining engineer, when she and her family moved to a silver mining town called Leadville in Colorado. Gambling was entrenched in the many mining camps of the Old West and, when Frank visited the gambling halls, Alice would join him. At first, she quietly studied the game and after a while began to play. In particular, she liked poker.

Sadly, Frank was killed in an explosion a few years into their marriage and poor Alice was left alone with no income. She decided to try earning a living with her gambling skills playing poker and faro. She was in demand as both a dealer and a player.

Alice was a natural beauty and, decked out in jewels and the latest fashions, her natural talent for the game created lots of attention. Around this time, she took up smoking cigars and began to travel from one mining camp to another. She built a reputation for herself until she met and married one of her opponents, Warren Tubbs, around 1890.

The couple moved to a ranch and had seven children. When Warren died of pneumonia in 1910, she had to pawn her wedding ring to pay for the funeral and afterwards went to a gambling parlor to earn the money to get it back. Faced with the same dilemma that she'd faced when she lost her first husband, Alice had to earn an income, so she left the ranch and went back to gambling.

Sometime later during Prohibition, Alice opened her own saloon, which provided gambling, liquor and also women who 'serviced' the customers. She maintained respect for her religious beliefs, so never opened on a Sunday. As time passed, Alice continued to operate her brothel but was arrested for shooting a man at her saloon (she was also often arrested for drunkenness and keeping a disorderly house). After many arrests for running the brothel, Alice was sentenced to prison and died in 1930 at the age of 79.

> Alice became known as 'Poker Alice', perhaps the most famous female gambler of the Old West. She claimed to have won more than $250,000 at the gaming tables (a major fortune for those times). One of Alice's favorite sayings was,
>
> "Praise the Lord and place your bets. I'll take your money with no regrets."

At my age I suppose I should be knitting. But I would rather play poker with five or six 'experts' than eat. – Alice Ivers Tubbs; aka Poker Alice

Akio Kashiwagi – 'The Whale'

Akio Kashiwagi was born in Imperial Japan in 1938 to a poor farming family. Having survived World War 2, Akio grew up rebellious and with a love of gambling, even though gambling was illegal in Japan.

He married a beautiful geisha and together they had three children. He established and operated a successful real estate and investment company but made more money from gambling.

He quickly became a legend in gambling circles because of the huge amounts of money he would bet in one hand, often $100,000 or $200,000. His favorite game was baccarat.

Those in the know called Akio a 'whale', a term for gamblers who bet hefty amounts. Casinos would give him credits well above the standard $1 million usually offered to whales and regulars.

Akio became so addicted to the thrill of gambling that he could gamble for 80 hours straight then collapse in his room to sleep until he was ready to start again.

Yes, Akio won a lot of money gambling but there was a darker side to it. Just like any other gambler, he would also often lose and look for ways to delay or avoid paying his gambling debts. This caught up with him when he was found murdered in his home in 1992, stabbed as many as 150 times with a samurai sword.

It is widely alleged that he was murdered by the Yakuza clan, a mafia-like crime syndicate in Japan, that he owed a lot of money to. After his death, it was discovered that he owed millions of dollars to casinos, including four million to Trump Plaza, and many of these casinos filed lawsuits to get their money back from his business.

Alice and Akio lived in different eras, different countries and different cultures, but they had one thing in common - they were hooked on gambling. Perhaps it came from trauma or perhaps it didn't, but what is certain is that, even though their compulsion to gambling caused major negative impacts on their lives – and in Akio's case, death - they wouldn't stop, and it's probable that they couldn't stop.

It's likely that they both created the habit of gambling because it was a feel-good thing, but the behavior eventually became unconscious and out of their control.

White Pigeon Ticket – Keno

Gambling is not a modern Western culture problem; it is inextricably linked to the history of humanity. In China, around 200 BC, 'White Pigeon Ticket' was played in gambling houses with the permission of the Province Governor. The Governor would receive a percentage of the profits, and the winnings were often used to fund state works.

The English translation for the game is *White Pigeon Ticket* because those who ran the games used white birds to notify the winners and send the winners' names throughout the country. Our modern lottos and keno now transport winners' names via our television and computer screens instead of white doves.

The legacy of *White Pigeon Ticket* remains in our society today. The game has evolved into what we now call keno, available in the majority of our modern gambling houses.

Playing Cards

It's believed that playing cards first appeared in China in the 9th century. The original cards bared little resemblance to those we use these days but, as card games spread throughout Europe, images of Kings and Queens appeared on them and evolved into the card decks we are more familiar with today.

Casinos

The first casinos, or gambling houses, appeared in Italy in the 17th century and casinos began to appear throughout the rest of Europe in the 19th century.

We're all familiar with the history of steamboats floating on the Mississippi River being used as gambling houses. These boats became the gambling venues for wealthy farmers and traders among the early settlers.

A form of poker has been around since 17th century Persia, and, as we've all seen portrayed in Hollywood blockbusters, it became the game to play on these floating casinos. Poker was known to be widely played in New Orleans around 1829.

Horse Racing

Since the beginning of recorded history, horse racing was an organized sport for all major civilizations around the globe.

The ancient Greek Olympics had events for both chariot and mounted horse racing. The sport was also very popular in the Roman Empire. Today, gambling on horse racing has evolved into a much wider sporting and gambling epidemic. We can gamble on dog races, human races, football, wrestling, boxing, cricket, basketball. If there's a sport, someone has set up a way to gamble on it.

Gambling probably predates money itself.

CHAPTER 7: GAMBLING – HOW TO TAKE BACK CONTROL

These days, technological advances have attracted a new generation of players. There are many opportunities for online gambling, with a growing trend of interaction between the social network and gambling.

As human beings, we are naturally competitive, we want to win, and gambling, in its many forms, offers us the 'sweet' promise of the chance to win. The language around gambling is now entrenched into our society from a young age. As children, we would 'bet' our friends that we would be first to the playground.

> Unlike substance abuse, gambling addiction is easily hidden from our sight and senses. You won't smell of cigarette smoke or be obviously inebriated. You don't get needle mark scars on your arms, nor will you put on copious amount of weight or have an allergic reaction or overdose. It is often a silent and invisible threat!

When treating clients for gambling addiction, I hear countless stories of people reaching a point where they feel unable to dig themselves out of a hole they've dug for themselves. They share their feeling of helplessness, the heaviness of a silent threat with no way out, so they dig deeper in the 'hope' that they can recoup their losses with one last bet.

I hear often, from both the gambler and their distraught loved ones, the stories of dishonesty, theft and secretiveness to their family and friends. The gambler often withdraws into a silent anxiety over their financial situation. They battle the habitual wiring in their brain that tells them, "If I just get that next big win, that will get me out of this mess."

Often the addicted gambler is in debt and has the constant threat of bankruptcy hovering over them. The only hope is that next gambling fix, that will 'fix' everything.

> *Just like every other addiction, gamblers have created a habit that can be easily broken with the 5-Step System.*

Gambling at first can be portrayed as glamorous, a source of connection and fun. In Australia, Melbourne Cup Day is widely celebrated and glamorized. Punters will spend weeks finding the perfect outfit, organizing parties and taking time off work to celebrate the annual horse racing event.

Gambling is glamorized by marketing messages. It is most often portrayed in terms of fun, friends, connection, happiness and relaxation.

People will travel from all over the world to visit casinos in Las Vegas 'to have fun.'

It's not surprising that some people who gamble once end up with a serious problem much later. It all began as an action that felt good, made them smile, laugh and connect. But, as I mentioned in Chapter 1, through reinforcement, a deep habit was created in the brain, and the gambler finds themselves with an addiction they feel little or no control over.

They don't intend to feed their rent or bill money into the poker or slot machines on Thursday night, but they end up doing just that because their unconscious wiring triggers the urge to keep seeking the pleasure and the pain of winning and, yes, even losing. The brain becomes addicted to the habit of the high and the low of gambling.

CHAPTER 7: GAMBLING – HOW TO TAKE BACK CONTROL

EXPERT INTERVIEW - Christopher Hunt

Christopher Hunt is a clinical psychologist at the Gambling and Research Clinic at the University of Sydney and primarily works with problem gamblers.

Christopher and his colleagues tend to avoid both the use of the word 'addiction' and the addiction model for gambling as they believe that gambling is distinct from drugs and alcohol in that the mechanism of action is quite different.

To treat a gambling client, Christopher believes that the solution is to tackle the challenge from the perspective of discovering what *entices* the client rather than what they are trying to escape from.

The fact that the client chooses this particular repetitive behavior says there is something that is drawing them to it.

According to Christopher and the team at the research clinic, the reason why people get caught up in gambling is more to do with gambling itself as opposed to some sort of underlying difficulty within the person.

"Sometimes there will be cases where there are significant underlying issues which make treatment for gambling considerably more difficult, but they definitely wouldn't represent the majority of cases," Christopher says.

The clinical evidence obtained at the clinic, as well as research evidence, supports this approach. However, the common view is still that gambling is reflective of some underlying trauma or some deep psychological issue from the past.

When Christopher started working at the clinic 12 years ago, 80% of clients were presenting with a problem with the poker or slot machines. Now these machines represent only 50%. There has been a clear shift, in Australia, for example, towards betting on horses and sports.

The commentary suggests that the view of poker or slot machines is that they are 'evil', but research suggests they were, until more recent times, simply the most widely available form of gambling. However, in the last five years or so, betting on sports has become widely marketed and accessible. You can now simply download one of the many sports betting apps on all your portable devices. You no longer need to find a venue to gamble on a slot machine. You can bet comfortably in the privacy of your own home, car, at your office desk, before the game, at the game or while on holiday.

Casinos

Only about 10% of clients present with a gambling challenge associated with gambling at casino tables. Baccarat is particularly popular with high rollers.

Casino table players experience another addictive element that other forms of gambling often don't deliver. At a blackjack, poker or baccarat table, for example, there are observers watching the players. For some players, the thrill of the pressure of being seen as the 'high roller', being able to lose large sums of money and walk away with your head held high, becomes the source of pleasure.

Casinos vet people who gamble large sums of money - the enticement of being recognized as a 'VIP' adds to the brain's chemical high. This added sense of importance plays directly into the human need for status. This sense of reward is far lower for slot or poker machine players, but often the pleasure can be experienced through the secrecy of that 'time-out' too.

CHAPTER 7: GAMBLING – HOW TO TAKE BACK CONTROL

Demographically, players at casinos are predominantly male and often from East Asian backgrounds, whereas poker or slot machine players are spread 50/50 in age, gender and all demographics.

According to Christopher, horse race punters tend to be older, and those who bet on sports in general tend to be younger men. Both Christopher and I often hear in our respective clinics from clients who have a problem gambling habit that they recall they had a win the very first time they gambled. Anecdotally, this seems to be the recurring theme with gamblers whose habit eventually ends up having a negative impact on their life.

The first win doesn't necessarily have to be a big win for it to take effect as a chemical 'high' in the brain. It could simply be that the punter risked $10 and won $20, but the seed is planted, underpinning the belief that you can win and the anticipation of 'hanging in there' to be a 'winner' again.

Essentially, what keeps gamblers chained to a slot machine or returning to place more bets is the notion that, because of the odds, surely "the win will eventually come".

This means that a slot machine player is more likely to stick with the game, even when losing, because the 'habitual' belief is that "the machine will eventually have to pay".

Those whose early associations with gambling have been of loss can think, "I've just won, so I'll walk away now", or "I've lost, and I don't want to keep losing, so I'll walk away."

This association that problem gamblers have between gambling and winning means that treatment can be easier than you think: we simply shift the gambler's attention to the link between the gambling and losing. When we rewire the brain to focus on the loss only, we break the trance and can change the habit.

Financial loss

The primary harm caused by problem gambling is financial harm, but this financial loss has the potential to create so many other personal losses. Losing great sums of money leads to the secondary harm of relationships. It can lead to problems at work or study because people become distracted and not focused on the tasks at work. And losing a lot of money can also cause psychological distress - people become anxious and depressed, which in turn leads to many other consequences. Illegal acts are also more common in gamblers than in the general population – for example, acts of fraud or 'borrowing' money from a friend or work. When this happens, I often hear the gambler say, "I just thought I'd have a win and put the money back." Their initial 'win' clouded their thought processes enabling them to think that they weren't stealing the money, just borrowing it.

Occasionally, Christopher will have a client involved in theft, fraud and embezzlement, but this is not the majority. Going bankrupt and losing everything such as car, house, and relationships are the other consequences we hear about in our clinics.

> For many clients, the problem with gambling isn't as extreme as I've mentioned above. For most, it means going without the everyday things - not being able to afford the doctor or the dentist or scraping by to pay for the weekly grocery bill, because their money is feeding the gambling industry.

The thing about gambling is that, when someone has no money, the 'habit' can appear to be broken but, when money becomes available again, the habit returns. Some would suggest that this means gambling is always within the gambler's control. However, it is my belief that the unconscious pattern (the habit) has to be broken in order for the gambler to become permanently free of the habit. There has to be a combination of choice and new brain wiring so that the triggers no longer feel overpowering. For the gambler to remain free of the habit, we need to empower them and rewire them with the new association of gambling to loss.

Christopher's approach works with clients through three steps.

The first step is to understand how they got to this position, to understand, as I've mentioned, their initial exposure to gambling and the development of the connection over time.

The second step is to focus on deconstructing these thoughts and explain how their choice of gambling really works. Most people actually have all sorts of misconceptions about how the odds play out.

The third step is to train people to apply what they now know to help them focus on the big picture when an urge to gamble is triggered.

How to actively choose not to gamble

How to apply that new knowledge in the real world is the key to overcoming the gambler's challenge.

It's crucial that someone learns how to have money and not gamble, even if they live next door to the trigger venue.

> When poker or slot machine clients are followed up six months to one to two years later, 75% to 85% report a significant reduction in the episodes of gambling and, indeed, many report no gambling at all.

No shame in asking for help

Both Christopher and I agree that the power comes from asking for help. Just pick up the phone and have a chat with someone.

CASE STUDY: Jean

Jean started playing poker machines at the age of 50. She had always liked dark, cavernous environments, and the pokie (slot machine) room was like that. It made her feel very comfortable.

Her work often involved helping people deal with grief, which was hard to deal with sometimes, and gambling gave her time out from thinking. When she was being honest, gambling gave her pleasure too. She started by betting 25-cent bets once per week, and she would sometimes win a little, which was exciting and thrilling.

Over the next 10 years, Jean's spending on the machines grew to the point where she was gambling up to $1,000 at a time, visiting the venues up to twice per week. Her losses averaged 75%. She would spend approximately $4,000 per month and on average win back about $1,500.

"I didn't mind at the time, because I could afford it," she told me.

Jean's mother had thought that way too, she reminisced. "Mum had been a big gambler on slot and poker machines and racehorses." She told me her mother would say, "I've won $50 on the horses," and Jean would say to her, "But you've lost $200."

Although Jean had not been raised by her mother, in the back of her mind she felt she had genetically inherited the addiction to gambling.

For 10 years, the amount of money Jean spent on her gambling had not caused undue pressure. Her justification was that, unlike other gamblers, she wasn't going into debt, and it wasn't causing any problems with relationships.

That all changed when a market fall caused major superannuation losses. Her savings that had been invested in a managed account were suddenly devastated too.

Jean now had a mortgage to pay with little income but the same expensive habit. She realized it had gone too far when she had to borrow money from a friend to get by.

Not only was it evident that she couldn't afford to gamble, but she felt dishonest because no-one knew that she gambled. Jean was still keeping her 'dirty little secret'.

At the time, Jean wasn't conscious of how incongruent she'd become. She was telling herself it was a harmless pleasure but, on the other hand, she was keeping it a secret. At the back of her mind, she thought the use of the money for gambling was immoral.

Before she came to see me in my clinic, Jean had tried several times to quit but she found it impossible. She could manage to stop for up to a month but then would see the pretty lights and flashing colors and it was just too much to resist. She logically understood the psychology of the attraction to the machines. She had witnessed over 10 years how the design of the machines had changed to meet the psychology of addiction, but she kidded herself into thinking that knowing that meant she could stop when she was ready.

Jean tried Gamblers Anonymous. She was wracked with guilt and shame and told people she was there as a therapist, that she wanted to study addiction and the psychology of gambling. After attending a few times, she decided it wasn't right for her and stopped going.

She told me, "In my mind, I didn't have the problems that other gamblers there had. I wasn't stealing to fund the addiction, like some people were." However, she was still gambling and couldn't stop.

Jean heard about me through a friend who had quit smoking after being treated by me. We began her treatment and, after one session, she noticed a shift in her thinking. She realized that, instead of an addiction, it was a habit. She had been telling herself that gambling was harmless but she was beginning to realize she'd been in denial. "I'd wanted to do what I wanted to do," she admitted.

Jean's treatment required three sessions. There has been an enormous shift in her perspective, and it has given her back control. It feels natural for her to no longer play the machines. Before her treatment, no matter how much willpower she used, she still felt like she had no control.

> At the time of writing this, Jean has now been free from gambling for six months and feels proud of herself. Her self-esteem has increased because she no longer judges herself for that 'dirty little secret' and for doing something she felt went against her morals.
>
> Now there is complete honesty and transparency with herself, and her friends and colleagues, she feels she's leading a life that is congruent and honest.

Jean's success in breaking free of her addiction gambling lies in the 5-Step System.

Step 1: Discovery

- Ask if the client actually WANTS to stop gambling. What is their 'why'? Uncover the specifics for each client – for example, which gambling game the client is drawn to and how often they play.
- What are their specific patterns or times when they gamble? Discover what the 'pain point' is for them in wanting to stop gambling – for example, is it the debt that stresses them, the guilt if they are lying and hiding the addiction from their family, or the problems it causes in their relationships? Is it their own shame or reflection?
- Then, uncover their language for how they would like to see themselves in the future – for example, free, in control, honest, financially secure. Also, question if there are links to their desire to quit in their relationships. Do they suffer from anxiety or depression? Are they on any medication? What, if any, are the indications for the addiction in their history?

Step 2: Decision Point

From the information discovered in Step 1, you will discover if there is past or present trauma underlying the addiction to gambling that will need to be addressed before addressing the addiction. However, it is rare for trauma to be at the root of gambling. Unless the gambling is linked to other addictions, it is usually simply a deep-seated habit that can be treated first.

Step 3: Expectations During and After Treatment

Manage the client's expectations of the session. This is explained in Chapter 4 on smoking.

Step 4: Treatment

The treatment is two hypnotherapy sessions over one to two weeks.

Step 5: Post-Treatment

Allowing the treatment to process will ensure the desire to be free of gambling will get stronger every day. It's important that you prepare the client to support themselves and not CHOOSE to gamble in the future. Old neural pathways can be reactivated and, later in life, bring back the habit, so it's important to prepare the client and equip them with the skills to focus on their freedom, the positive outcomes and benefits. Even though the intensity of urges will diminish with time, it's important to equip the client with skills to reframe or divert the brain's attention to the positivity of being free.

Gambling is endemic in modern society, so having the confidence to work with the gambling habit will empower your clients and become a skill that is an asset for your business.

In the following chapter, I address the addiction to the habit of using drugs, both recreational and harder drugs.

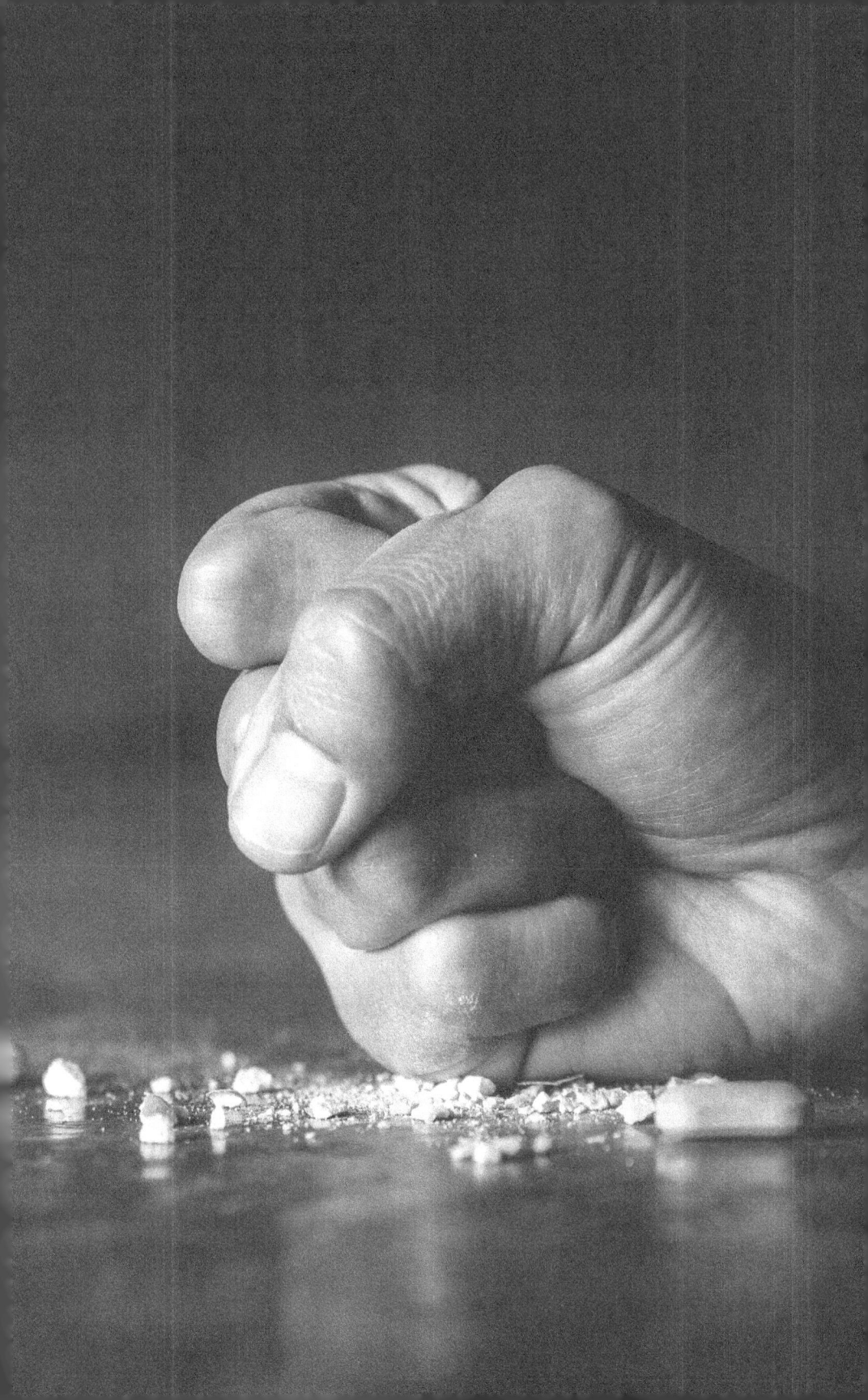

CHAPTER 8
Drugs – How to Kick the Habit

Here's the thing - society may have changed in the last 60,000 years or so, but the fascination with getting high has remained constant.

According to Phil Withington, Professor of History at the University of Sheffield, and one of the world's leading historians of intoxicants and intoxication, there is archaeobotanical evidence of the consumption of ephedra and cannabis in Neolithic and Bronze Age Europe (around 12,000 years ago). There is also evidence of entoptic imagery in Upper Paleolithic artwork (produced during altered states of consciousness) as far back as 40,000 years ago.

According to Ryan Riley, a Graduate Student Researcher at North Carolina State University who studies the history and anthropology of ancient pharmacology with a specific emphasis on psychotropic substances, our primate ancestors have enjoyed the dizzying, physiological effects of fermented fruits for tens of millions of years.

> In 2500 BC, people in Mesopotamia referred to opium as the 'joy plant', and we know that hallucinogenic mushrooms have been used in ancient Siberia, and also in Central and South America, for thousands of years.
>
> Until the 19th century, drugs were mostly used for religious purposes and spiritual experiences.

CHAPTER 8: DRUGS – HOW TO KICK THE HABIT

Just the idea that you'd sit around and take drugs... apart from alcohol... it would be more of a 19th century kind of idea. – Richard Miller, Professor of Pharmacology, Northwestern University and the author of <u>Drugged: The Science and Culture Behind Psychotropic Drugs</u>

Before 1914, cocaine was legal

Queen Victoria, Thomas Edison and Ulysses S. Grant were all fans of cocaine in the form of a famous drink at the time called Vin Mariani, which was essentially wine laced with cocaine. This drink was even promoted by Pope Leo XIII, who awarded the drink an official medal from the Vatican. He claimed that he kept the drink in a personal hip flask to "fortify himself when prayer was insufficient".

◇◇◇

Queen Victoria, Thomas Edison and Ulysses S. Grant were all fans of cocaine in the form of a famous drink at the time called Vin Mariani, which was essentially wine laced with cocaine. This drink was even promoted by Pope Leo XIII, who awarded the drink an official medal from the Vatican.

◇◇◇

The inventor of this drink, a French chemist by the name of Angelo Mariani, billed the drink as a 'health tonic' and spent a fortune at the time on campaigning and advertising it. Just like the meteoric acceptance of cigarettes as a health product, normalizing it for women and men alike, or the branding of junk food through the media today, the campaigning of this drink played a huge part in the popularity of Vin Mariani.

Vin Mariani was promoted for all the reasons people now pursue cocaine in modern times:

- to provide you with energy
- to motivate you
- to reduce hunger
- to stimulate you
- to provide clarity and alertness

But, like cocaine in its pure form, there was a downside: many people became addicted to the drink. It was also given to children to cure ailments when it was, in fact, killing them.

John Belushi

John Belushi, comedian, movie star and voted the greatest of *Saturday Night Live*s 145-cast members in 2015 by *Rolling Stone* magazine, passed away on the 5th of March 1982 from a drug overdose.

Sadly, he is now remembered more for his drug addiction (cocaine, in particular,) rather than his comedic genius. His co-star in *The Blues Brothers*, Dan Ackroyd, has spoken out about how much Belushi loved cocaine.

> "We had a budget in the movie for cocaine for night shoots. Everyone did it, including me. Never to excess, and not ever to where I wanted to buy it or have it. [But] John, he just loved what it did. It sort of brought him alive at night, that superpower feeling where you start to talk and converse and figure you can solve all the world's problems."
> — Dan Ackroyd

At the time of his death, Belushi's drug-fueled lifestyle was spiraling completely out of control. He had even hired a bodyguard to keep him away from drugs. He was spending $2,500 per week on drugs and getting more and more behind on a movie script he was working on. He died from a 'speedball injection' – a combination of heroin and cocaine.

Cocaine

Cocaine, a derivative of the cocoa plant, is one of the most powerfully addictive drugs of abuse. It's a stimulant drug that causes its users to feel euphoric. No individual can predict whether their next dose will prove fatal. In fact, if a person is using cocaine recreationally, they are at a high risk of overdose.

Statistics provided by the National Center for Health Statistics in America show that drug overdose deaths involving cocaine went from 3,822 in 1999 to 13,942 in 2017.

Until 2013, there was little difference between deaths from cocaine combined with an opioid and deaths from cocaine without any opioid. Since 2014, the number of deaths has increased significantly and has been driven mainly by deaths involving cocaine in combination with other synthetic narcotics.

When first taking cocaine, the user will usually feel euphoric, energetic, talkative and mentally alert. Their sight, sound and touch will be ultrasensitive, but these effects will last less and less each time the drug is used, which leads to a need for more cocaine more often to generate the same level of stimulation.

Cocaine addicts will find that those wonderful feelings that got them addicted to cocaine in the first place begin to disappear altogether and, instead, they are experiencing anxiety, paranoia and depression.

Other areas of their life also begin to be impacted negatively - such as their health, relationships, social life, financial situation and career - but, by then, it's such a deep habit that it feels impossible to stop.

Cocaine – Andy's story

Andy started using cocaine when he was 24, but the path to cocaine started much earlier.

Hanging out with an older group of kids, Andy first smoked pot at 13 and drank alcohol at 15. His next steps were speed, then ecstasy and eventually getting into cocaine because it was the social or cool thing to do. People in his scene were using it and it was in all the pubs and clubs he went to.

To be honest, he liked the effects, and coming down from cocaine the next day was not as bad as coming down from ecstasy or speed. Also, he could drink more alcohol without getting drunk when he was using cocaine.

There were four years in his 20s, however, when Andy stopped taking all drugs. He was playing professional football and simply quit during the time. In his mid-30s, after he finished his football career, things began spiraling out of control.

Andy was making good money, but the more he earned the more cocaine he'd take. He was using about three grams of cocaine every day. Plus, he began to hang out with people who also had disposable incomes. There was always plenty of cocaine available. He could take it at his leisure without thinking twice about it.

CHAPTER 8: DRUGS – HOW TO KICK THE HABIT

It wasn't long before Andy relied on cocaine to feel good or, when life wasn't going the way he wanted it to, he used it to escape.

Over the ensuing years, staying awake at night and spending large amounts of money on cocaine caused relationships to fail. The effects of the drug and the lifestyle caused Andy to become unfit and unhealthy.

Starting in 2014, Andy tried to clean up and spent time in a variety of detox centers. Unfortunately, this started a cycle of getting clean and then using again.

Sometimes he'd manage to go straight for a few weeks after detoxing before relapsing. Sometimes Andy would use cocaine for four or five days without any sleep and then spend four or five days recovering. It was a vicious cycle.

By the time Andy booked in to see me in 2019, the habit and lifestyle had all become too much for him. He was emotionally, physically and mentally wrecked. Some days he would only get out of bed to drink alcohol and snort cocaine.

He didn't even get a high from cocaine anymore. He became paranoid thinking there were people outside waiting for him. He was embarrassed to see people when he was under the influence. But, as soon as the cocaine started to wear off, he would need more, and this made him frustrated and angry.

Andy didn't spend time with his young son, and he was spending $180,000 annually on his habit. If he continued on this path, he knew he would lose his business and his relationship.

After his one-session treatment with me, Andy wasn't sure if it had worked. When he left my office, he didn't feel any different. So, being the type of person who wanted evidence, he decided he'd test it out. He went to the pub with friends who had cocaine. He realized he felt in control and really didn't want it.

He went home to his partner and told her, "I'm cured! It's a miracle!" After trying to quit for four years using a variety of different methods and programs, Andy couldn't believe that the whole thought process about cocaine had disappeared instantly!

At the time of writing this book, Andy has been free of the cocaine habit for nearly two years. He's had many opportunities to use cocaine, but he is no longer interested in it. He spends quality time with his son and partner, his business is thriving, despite the industry slowing down in general, and he is back at the gym and eating healthy again.

Andy looks the picture of good health. He feels mentally clear and is back out in the world loving life. Andy is loving life clean.

The problem with pot

Cannabis has been around since the dawn of time. When we think of Jamaica, we think of marijuana but, surprisingly, marijuana has actually been illegal in Jamaica for the most part of the past 100 years. Even so, its use was customary from the 1850s, when it was first imported from East India by indentured servants during the time when Britain ruled both nations. India's influence on marijuana in Jamaica is evident with common terms such as 'ganja', which is a Hindi word meaning 'hemp' or 'hemp resin'.

It was in the 1920s when a black religious consciousness movement known as Rastafari came into the islands. The emergence of Rastafarian culture cemented the culture of marijuana in Jamaica. It is used for spiritual and religious reasons among Rastafarians, just as other drugs have been over the history of time.

The famous singer/songwriter, Bob Marley, became an advocate of marijuana. In 1966, he converted from Catholicism to become a Rastafarian and was the source of many famous quotes in support of marijuana such as, *"When you smoke the herb, it reveals you to yourself."*

But there's good and bad in everything in different quantities for different people. Like other drugs, marijuana has many negative side effects, if you become reliant on it. It can make a user become introverted, slow down reaction time, produce anxiety and panic attacks, and cause memory loss and paranoia. It can also cause problems with relationships, finances and productivity.

Party drugs

The emergence of the rave scene saw party goers switch from alcohol to party drugs, such as ecstasy and speed, both of which keep the partygoer energized, happy and dancing all night, 'feeling the love' - that experience of 'an enhanced state of consciousness'.

Raves originated in Chicago as an underground movement where dance music enthusiasts would dance for hours to all types of electronic music. It wasn't long before the concept spread around the world.

The highs and the lows

After such an intense high from popping a pill, there is going to be a comedown affecting mood, health and mental state. There have been people who have partied so hard on party drugs for an extended period that it has had a permanent negative effect on their life, including their brain.

Unfortunately, party drugs can also be lethal. You can never be 100% sure what you are consuming. There has been a lot of publicity around party drugs over the years due to young people taking a fatal pill while attending a rave.

Ice

EXPERT INTERVIEW - Julian Docherty

One of the biggest drug problems throughout the Western world, and definitely in Australia today, is ice.

According to Julian from Pathways, in the past, a client would be using cannabis and occasionally other drugs, but nowadays ice is the prime substance they use.

More often than not, it's people between 18 to 25 years who are using ice as their only drug source. And it is in large quantities.

Julian says, "Some young people I see are using up to one and a half grams every day."

Some individuals might be okay using these large amounts, but it is more likely that the user would be constantly fluctuating between euphoria and paranoia or be suffering from auditory hallucinations.

CHAPTER 8: DRUGS – HOW TO KICK THE HABIT

The definition of a problem is when something is negatively impacting on other areas of your life. For ice users, it will be a slow progression, often starting by hanging out with people who are worse off than you and, once you become the worst, you find a new group until you become the worst in that group.

During this progression, ice users are losing their jobs, their relationships, families and connections. Sometimes they might lose their home and their children.

Some people who are struggling with ice addiction come from a background of trauma, but not always. Julian has seen people who have come from seriously traumatic backgrounds become ice addicts and he has seen people who come from good families, who attended good schools and who have never suffered from severe trauma also become serious ice addicts.

He believes it is how someone copes with life that will determine the intensity of an addiction. When a person is growing up, there is no manual saying, "Well, if this happens, this is what you do."

Ice is addictive because of the quantity of dopamine and endorphins that get released into the brain when it's used.

Julian states, "Once a person has used large quantities of ice, it causes a chemical imbalance in the brain. They find the only time they can enjoy themselves and be happy is when they are on ice." He adds, "When they withdraw from the drug, they find they are sad and depressed. To overcome the addiction, they have to stay off stimulants to give the receptors in their brain time to repair themselves."

Like clients who attend Pathways for alcohol addiction, clients who want to get off ice attend a 12-week program with psychoeducational group sessions. Clients are asked not to attend under the influence so, by not using that morning and throughout that day, they start to see that, in small steps, they can break free.

As well as being educated throughout the program, clients are given a safe environment where they can connect with others who also want to get clean and sober.

Group sessions include minimizing harm, drug education and relapse prevention tips and strategies.

Cold Turkey

When someone stops using ice cold turkey, they become lethargic and want to sleep. Over this period, their body will get used to daily habits again, such as eating properly.

They will have intense cravings for ice and Julian will advise them that it's okay if their mind starts to think about using but it's not okay to feed that thought by staying focused on it. And it's not okay to act on it.

If a passing thought is entertained long enough, such as, "Oh, I might go and use," it will trigger the brain to activate full cravings. The impulsive decision to go and use is harder to manage for most at the beginning.

The most effective way for clients to quit ice successfully is to detox first in a residential setting and then follow through with the therapy and support they need.

The scariest part of any person breaking free from ice, particularly if they are young, is having to leave behind everyone they knew associated with ice and having to start again finding new, sober friends and building relationships. Often, they find it very challenging, and this can often cause a relapse.

Heroin

I don't think anyone could forget the disturbing scene in the harrowing 1996 film 'Trainspotting', where Allison is screaming when she discovers her baby dead in its crib. Bundled in dirty blankets, the viewer speculates that Allison must have been lost in a heroin-induced stupor for a long time for this to happen, highlighting the dangers of the drug.

Breaking free of heroin can be dangerous. Like other addictions, not everybody who takes heroin becomes addicted to it but, for those who do, it is advised that they seek professional help and don't try and quit alone.

Tolerance levels can kill after quitting and relapsing

The most dangerous time to fatally overdose from heroin is after quitting cold turkey and then relapsing because users don't take into account that their tolerance will be lower than before.

Physical symptoms of coming off heroin include:

- nausea and vomiting
- goosebumps
- bone aches
- abdominal cramping
- cold sweats
- diarrhea

For some people, they literally can't function day to day while coming off heroin.

The psychological effects of heroin addiction can include:

- insomnia
- tremors
- restlessness
- anxiety
- intense cravings
- agitation
- difficulty concentrating
- fatigue
- difficulty finding pleasure in normal life

By the time a client needs help breaking free from heroin addiction, they have created a highly traumatic event in their life, and it is likely that the reason they became so addicted in the first place was because of another trauma. I'll talk more about trauma in the next chapter.

Psychosis

Differentiating drugs into different categories, depending on whether they are hard core or not, is difficult. Marijuana is now legal in many parts of the world, yet it can cause psychosis in some people. Alcohol is socially acceptable, yet it can also cause psychosis.

Psychosis is a severe mental disorder in which thoughts and emotions are so impaired that contact is lost with external reality. It may occur as a result of a psychiatric illness (for example, bipolar or schizophrenia), a health condition, medication or drug abuse.

Prolonged use of drugs, including alcohol, can manifest psychotic symptoms and ongoing mental illness.

Hunter's story

Hunter was 21 years old and had been smoking marijuana every day for four years. It had got to the point where he had to quit his job in the family business because it required driving and he was now working as a packer in a warehouse instead.

Marijuana didn't mellow him out as it did his friends. Instead, it pumped him up. It became frightening when he found himself hallucinating. He heard angry and demanding voices inside his head telling him he was worthless and to kill himself.

An ambulance was called and Hunter was hospitalized for a week and diagnosed with schizophrenia. With the help of antipsychotic medication, he slowly came out of the psychosis.

For as long as he smoked marijuana, he was going to experience psychosis. It was a struggle to break free from his addiction, but he has now been marijuana free for two years. Hunter only discovered how my treatment could help him recently, so my work with him has been for PTSD and healing.

Hunter's story is an example of how a drug that is thought of by many as harmless can actually, for some, cause the onset of psychosis and mental illness.

Recently, I have worked with a client who has a long history of abusing cocaine, alcohol, marijuana and prescription medication. He first came to me to quit smoking, which worked extremely effectively, and then he came back a few months later after a psychotic episode when drinking alcohol.

The psychotic episode was only brief and his treatment was working on the underlying trauma and cutting out alcohol and drugs. During the program, we saw great success but, after experiencing an excruciating and traumatic dental problem, he began taking the prescription medication he'd been prescribed. Unfortunately, this caused a brief psychosis and a nervous breakdown. After a further session, which helped him relax and gave him some clarity, I advised him to continue working with me but to also get further advice for mental illness.

Drugs – The 5-Step System

This is how I worked with Andy, Hunter and others using cocaine, marijuana and ice to help them break habitual addictions.

Step 1: Discovery

This step is all about discovering what the client's life is like - what is their family set up, and their history?

- Do they suffer from anxiety, depression, past or present trauma?
- When did they become addicted to the drug?
- How often do they use it and when?
- Why do they want to quit?
- What negative effect is it causing mentally, physically and emotionally?
- Have they tried to quit in the past?
- What have they tried?

- What benefits are they looking forward to once they are free of the addiction?
- Do they really want to quit, or is there another agenda?

Step 2: Decision Point

Decide whether or not the drug habit is a symptom of a deeper trauma.

Step 3: Managing expectations

The experience of hypnotherapy, as described in Chapter 4.

Step 4: Treatment

If the drug use is a symptom of a deeper trauma, then treat the trauma first. If not, then start with a hypnotherapy session to break the habit.

Step 5: Post-Treatment

Help the client with tools to stop CHOOSING to take the drug. Help them understand the consequences, educate them about how the brain learns and gets triggered back to reactivating old neural pathways that cause cravings and connections to the drug. I always ask them to contact me if there is *any* struggle after the treatment. I give them a realistic expectation to empower them to make the healthy choice - "You are made up of different parts and it means there is a part of you that still wants to keep the habit." I ensure they know that, if that part becomes triggered, they can return to address it in the next session.

What came first - the chicken or the egg?

It can be difficult to tell whether mental illness causes drug abuse or drug abuse causes mental illness. As I mentioned in Chapter 1, I was no longer anxious when I drank alcohol, and it is common that people will often start enjoying alcohol or marijuana because it helps them feel calm or relaxed rather than anxious and self-conscious.

People suffering a mental illness are more likely to turn to drugs to help them feel better. On the other hand, there is evidence that drug abuse can trigger mental illness. Studies suggest that 50% of people with a mental illness have a drug or alcohol problem.

In Chapter 9, I'll discuss how we sometimes need to address the trauma underlying the addiction before we can start to address an addiction or a habit.

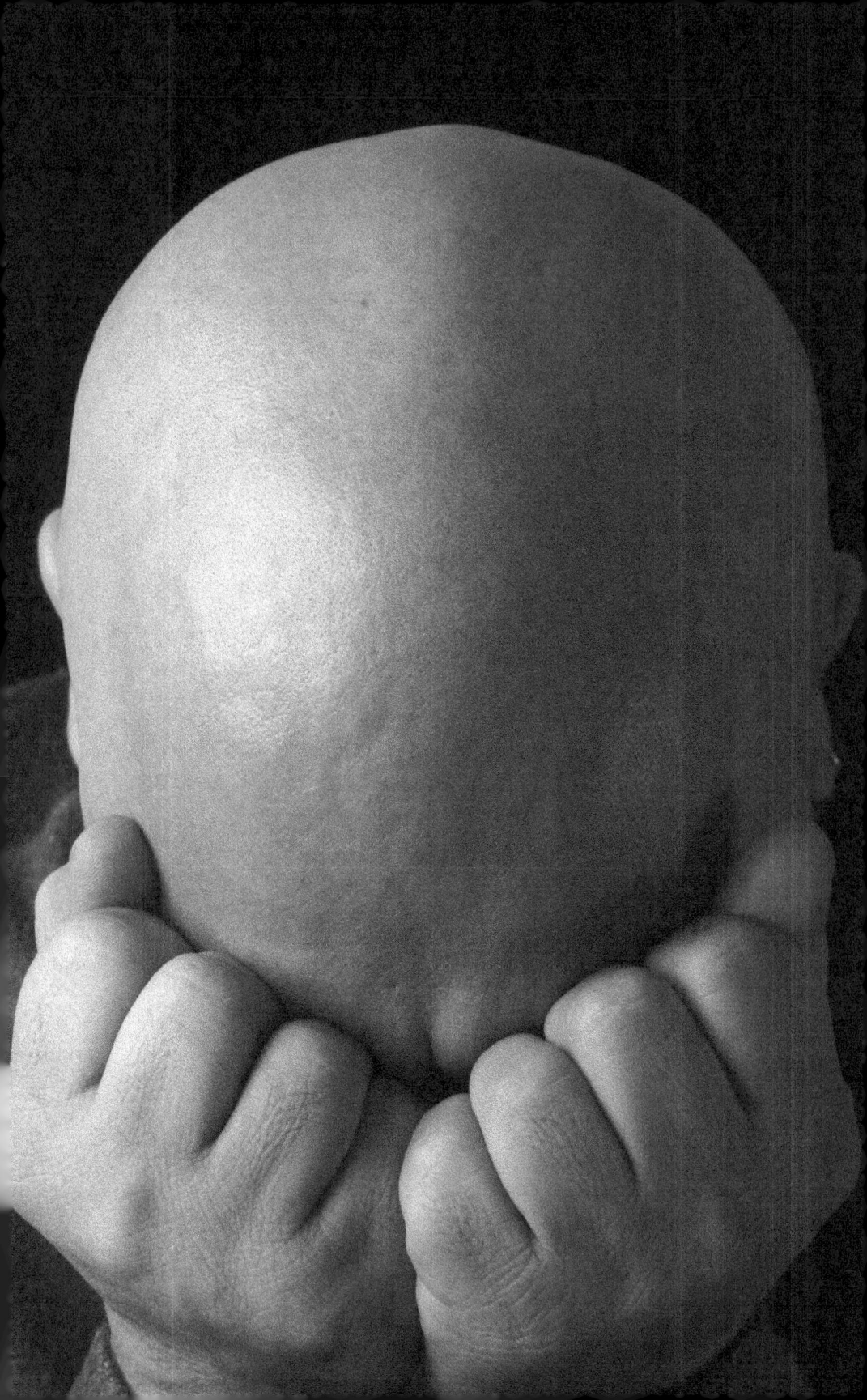

CHAPTER 9

If Trauma Gets in the Way of Breaking an Addiction

I lived with my mother until I was two years old – that is when my brother, Terry, who is seven years older than me, and I were taken away because she was an 'unfit mother'.

I saw my mother only a handful of times during my childhood, so I felt very disconnected from her. As I mentioned in the introduction, growing up in 1940s and 1950s New Zealand, she became lost in the New Zealand social welfare system.

I often ponder that with the right treatment and support, perhaps my mother might have recovered. She was severely traumatized from a violent and abusive childhood. She was the middle child of three sisters and, at a very young age, the three girls were taken from their parents, Bob and Mary Miller, and placed into separate foster homes. My grandmother, Mary, went into a psychiatric hospital.

> **My cousin Shayne writes in his biography:**
>
> *"I was helping my cousin Terry sort through Aunt Nat's belongings on the day of her cremation. Her room at the psychiatric hospital was full of papers and obscure journals and sadly little else.*
>
> *There was a thick manila folder full of documents, and when I flicked through the pages, it became apparent that these were my aunt's welfare files.*
>
> *Sadness in bland typewriter script, secrets made official. As if by serendipity, I stopped on a particular sheet and written there were the words, "sexually abused by father along with older sister. Dirty Bob Miller having his way with the kids."*

CHAPTER 9: IF TRAUMA GETS IN THE WAY OF BREAKING AN ADDICTION

Unfortunately, my mother was not only sexually abused by her father but also abused by a series of foster fathers. Mum smoked 40 cigarettes per day from the day she turned 18 until the day she died. I went to visit her once when she was attempting to quit, and she was sitting on the front step under one of the many 'no smoking' signs that she had placed around the house. She was puffing away.

Mum's addiction was cigarettes, Aunty Ricci's was alcohol.

When I was living with Aunty Ricci as a teenager, I spent many nights keeping her company while she talked and poured herself one glass of wine after the other. I felt increasingly uncomfortable as she drank, but I was too polite to leave and, because I loved her, I also wanted to please her.

Later in her life, I would strategically make phone calls to her in the morning hoping to speak to her before the first glass had been poured.

Both mother and Aunty Ricci were extremely talented and had big loving hearts and wicked senses of humor but, sadly, they were consumed by their own trauma. Both women passed away from massive heart attacks in their 60s.

Mum and Aunty Ricci's addictions were clearly a symptom of deeper core issues – traumatic life events that, with hindsight and skills, could have been addressed. The trauma they each experienced not only occurred during their childhoods but also manifested into adulthood. Neither of them lived in a time where trauma was understood or addressed. Neither of them had the chance to heal. The risk of heart disease is increased significantly from alcohol and cigarettes, but I often wonder if they died from broken hearts?

I loved them both, and now I love the fact that I can help others change what my mother and Aunty Ricci couldn't.

Mark's story

Mark wanted to stop smoking marijuana. He was smoking from the moment he woke until he went to bed at night. He couldn't work and felt chained to the house because of the dependence. Over time, he had become introverted and had lost confidence.

Marijuana affected his mental, physical and emotional capacity. He had no appetite, a terrible cough and emphysema and felt physically weak. He was moody, anxious, angry and always had a foggy brain.

Mark had grown up in an abusive home and, as an adult, he had joined a cult which resulted in his losing everything, including his remaining family. Later, after being bashed during a robbery, he suffered a stroke on the operating table and had to learn to walk and talk again. This all culminated in the perfect storm - he had lost everything and now his dream of a career as a pilot was gone too.

I advised Mark that, by addressing past trauma, he would be more likely to get a lasting result. It seemed that his dependency on marijuana had become a solution to the trauma. Mark, however, chose to initially try working on breaking the habit without addressing the trauma. He wanted to see how we went first.

CHAPTER 9: IF TRAUMA GETS IN THE WAY OF BREAKING AN ADDICTION

After the initial session, even though Mark didn't fully stop using marijuana, he used less and, importantly, noticed a huge positive difference within himself, his mood and his outlook. From this more positive and hopeful headspace, Mark decided he now felt ready to see me to work on the trauma.

After five further sessions, Mark felt transformed. He was no longer getting angry or anxious, and he was reaching out to family members confidently and rebuilding relationships. He felt lighter, happier and more motivated. His thinking was clearer.

Even though he was still reliant on smoking for the moment, marijuana was just a bad habit, it felt easier. I was now able to do a session with him on breaking the habit of smoking marijuana for good.

Mark succeeded. He now has his life back. He has reconnected with his son who he'd been estranged from for many years. He has started his own business and is feeling fitter and healthier and is eating properly. He says, "I feel confident to be back out in the world fully living life." Mark is happy and at peace.

As seen in the example of Mark, the treatment of hypnotherapy is a very powerful modality to heal trauma.

The 5-Step System still applies for clients who have an underlying trauma associated with their habit or addiction. The only difference is at Step 4 where the treatment is to use a number of trauma release sessions (the number is dependent on the client and their journey) to address the trauma.

Once someone is ready to move forward, I return my focus to treat the addiction. This is based on the client's pace and progress. We can then view the addiction to the habit as simply an unwanted habit that can easily be broken with hypnosis.

As I bring this book to a close, I provide a number of ways to prepare people for their path forward free from the habit or addiction. In the following chapter, I have provided my *Freedom Prescriptions*. There is a prescription for each habit and addiction I addressed in the book.

You'll also read about my 'moment'! This moment was the tipping point that offered me two paths. It offered me the choice to peel away my own strangler fig and set myself free, despite my upbringing and a genetic predisposition for addiction. In spite of the hardships and losses, the rejection and the fears of my earlier life, I too faced a moment that presented me with two paths - the path of addiction, loss, sadness and rejection, or the path of empowered choice and freedom.

Can you guess which one I chose?

CHAPTER 10

Take Control and Gain Freedom

The King's Parable

This is my interpretation of a parable that has been passed down through the ages.

There was a king who said to the court sages, "I have a ring with one of the finest diamonds in the world. I want to hide a message under the diamond that will be useful in situations of extreme despair."

He continued to his faithful servants, "I will give this ring to my heirs and it will serve them faithfully." He demanded that his court sages make the message very short so that it could be placed under the diamond.

The sages knew how to write treaties but did not know how to express themselves in one short sentence. They thought and thought but did not come up with a solution.

The king complained of their failure to a faithful old servant who had raised him as an infant and was part of the family. The old man said to the king, "I am not a sage, I am not educated, but I know such a message. Many years I have spent in the palace and I have met many people. Long ago, I served a visiting mystic whom your father invited to the kingdom. This mystic gave me a message written on a miniature sacred scroll."

The old servant requested of the king, "Do not read the message now, but save it under the diamond in your ring and only open the message when there's no way out at all."

The king listened to the old servant and had the sacred miniature scroll placed under the diamond in his ring.

After some time, the enemies attacked the country and the king was losing the war. He fled on his horse and his enemies pursued him. He was alone, his enemies were many. He rode to the end of the road. There was a huge deep cliff before him. If he fell, it would be the end. He could not go back, as the enemies were approaching. He could hear the pounding of their horses' hooves. He had no way out. He was in complete despair.

And then he remembered the ring. He removed the diamond and opened the scroll to read the inscription. It said, "This too shall pass."

After reading the message, everything became quiet. The deafening sound of the horses disappeared. The enemy had taken the wrong path and become lost.

The king was filled with gratitude to the servant and the unknown mystic. The words were powerful. He replaced the diamond and set out on the road. He gathered his army and returned to his kingdom.

On the day when he returned to the palace, they arranged a magnificent feast for his subjects – his people loved their king. The king was happy and proud.

The old servant came up to him and said softly, "Even in this moment, look at the message again."

The King said, "Now I am a winner, people are celebrating my return. I'm not in despair, not in a hopeless situation."

"Listen to this old servant," the servant replied. "The message works not only in moments of despair, but also in moments of victory."

The king read the message again, "This too shall pass."

And again, he felt a silence fall over him, although he was in the midst of a noisy dancing crowd. His pride dissolved. He understood the message. He was a wise man.

And then the old man said to the king, "Do you remember everything that has ever happened to you? No event, feeling or thought is permanent. As night changes to day, so too do moments of joy and despair replace each other. Accept both negative and positive experiences as the nature of things, as part of life."

The Parable of Overcoming Habits and Addictions

Overwhelmingly, clients who follow my 5-Step System achieve tremendous success.

Their success is often accompanied by pleasant surprise and astonishing disbelief! This is usually because, by the time they come to see me, they have tried so many methods to quit that they have almost given up trying to give up.

I receive positive feedback, even years later, from clients who are still free and in control. And, of course, they would be because the 5-Step System doesn't 'wear off'.

Usually the only way someone might relapse is if they CHOOSE to indulge in their past habit and allow triggers to resurface by ignoring what they've learned from our sessions or this book.

Sometimes the person allows everyday challenges to overwhelm them and they consciously surrender to the old addiction to the habit. Or in moments of cockiness, where overconfidence surpasses rational thought, they surrender to the habit. In this situation, clients tell me they say to themselves, "Just one won't hurt... I'll do it this once. I'll be alright."

We can liken the moment that we cave in to the trigger to the moment that the king stood at the cliff's edge. The king had a choice to make, just like we do:

- to either read the parable under the diamond, or
- to ignore it.

In the case of habits and addictions, we either:

- use the strategies we've learned in this book, which allows the trigger, pang, craving or urge to pass, or
- ignore the strategies and cave in, surrendering to the addiction to the habit once again.

Every craving, urge, pang, impulse, trigger, desire, need or discomfort that yearns for that habitual thought, action or substance, will pass.

A craving – this too shall pass.
An urge – this too shall pass.
A trigger or yearning – this too shall pass.
A pang or impulse... when a conscious choice is made to do something different, this too shall pass.

No therapist can take away someone's freedom of choice to smoke, drink or gamble; to take drugs or to eat sugar but, when the client chooses to, they tell their unconscious mind that they want that habit in their life and, therefore, their unconscious mind will support that decision.

Most often, relapse happens because someone thinks something like "one time won't hurt".

Perhaps being out with friends and others who are smoking cigarettes - and even though they feel completely in control and could easily say "no, thank you" - they make that decision of "one won't hurt".

But, as soon as they have that 'one', they discover that they are once again out of control and craving cigarettes. They have brought back the old habit. Or they could be in a similar situation with friends taking drugs or drinking alcohol. With food, it could be a matter of consistently going against their newly formed habits of eating clean, healthy food and ultimately overriding it.

If you, or your client, experiences a relapse, a one-off session will be sufficient to be free and in control once more.

On rare occasions, there will be more going on than simply choosing to indulge in the old outdated habit. It will be because the person didn't have the tools to cope with whatever stress or emotion was being felt at that time and had been relying on willpower as their coping mechanism.

Yes, we have disconnected the trigger to stress and you, or your client, know how wonderful it has been to be free of the old 'go to' every time there is stress. But this time has been different for some reason. It could be that you, or your client, are suffering anxiety and have mistaken it for a craving. It could be that stress is being used as an excuse to not support yourself or, if it's your client, then themselves (remember – there must be that desire to want to quit). It could be that a trauma has been reactivated from the past which didn't impact the initial treatment or a new traumatic experience has occurred. Overwhelmingly, most of my clients find that no stress/trauma-related event would cause them to relapse, but it can happen and it can also be resolved.

In our unconscious mind, we are made up of many different parts. If someone relapses, it means that there is a part in the unconscious mind that is still attached to keeping the habit. Perhaps it's because on one level it keeps them feeling safe.

Therefore, if a client relapses, or even if they are just struggling, I will work on 'that part' that is still attached to the habit. This is a very powerful way to eliminate the habit once and for all.

If it's not working, then either they don't want to quit or trauma that wasn't getting in the way before is now getting in the way. As explained in Chapter 9, in this case, we must work on resolving the trauma first.

What it usually boils down to is this:

1. They used free will.

In order not to repeat the habit again, this question must be answered, "Do they want to keep the habit or lose it?" If the choice is to lose it, then it is important to have support moving forward. They can choose to remember that 'this too shall pass', if they contemplate venturing down that path again - a brief moment of self-talk to say 'stop'. They are choosing personal responsibility.

2. They are stressed.

There are many tools to support oneself during stressful times that will be far more enduring than reverting back to the old habit. I have provided my *Freedom Prescription* for each habit or addiction that we have addressed in this book.

Each *Freedom Prescription* is a strategy that you or your client can follow to minimize the impact of stress, which can trigger the old pattern. (Especially useful in the early days after choosing to shake off that strangler fig as the brain adjusts and rewires the new, healthier patterns of choice.)

Mix and match any of these prescriptions to discover what resonates best for you or for your client.

FREEDOM PRESCRIPTION FOR SMOKING	
Prescription	Remove yourself from the situation: • go for a walk around the block. • go for a drive. • go into another room.
Do one thing different:	• Have a glass of water and focus mindfully on the water, the temperature, the sensation of the water as it is swallowed, the relief quenching that thirst. • Put a timer on for three minutes and focus on your breathing… breathing in for one, two, three and out … two, three. • Walk outside and eat an apple, focus on the apple until it is finished. • Focus on the mantra from the parable as you breathe in and out, "this too shall pass," because it will.

	FREEDOM PRESCRIPTION FOR FOOD
Prescription	Step 1: Visualization: Close your eyes and take in a deep breath… Imagine the freedom part of you compared to the craving part. Visualize the food you're craving in one hand, giant in size and taking up all the space. Then visualize the freedom part of you - that part that is free, in control, healthy, slim, vital, confident and happy and all the things you want to be. Imagine for the moment the freedom part of you as quite small. Then imagine, or pretend, that the freedom part starts to grow bigger and bigger and see the food craving shrinking smaller and smaller. Once the freedom part is as big as you can make it, slap the hand with the freedom part down onto the hand with the craving part and notice the craving disappears. (With practice, this will take less than a few seconds to complete.)
Remember to do one thing different:	• Have a glass of water and focus mindfully on the water, the temperature, the sensation of the water as it is swallowed, the relief quenching that thirst. • Put a timer on for three minutes and focus on your breathing… breathing in for one, two, three and out … two, three. • Walk outside and eat an apple, focus on the apple until it is finished. • Focus on the mantra from the parable as you breathe in and out, "this too shall pass," because it will.

	FREEDOM PRESCRIPTION FOR ALCOHOL
Prescription	• Write down the three main positive reasons for wanting to be free from alcohol. • Close your eyes and imagine that you throw a bottle, or a glass, of the alcohol of your choice against a wall. Or using all your energy to take control by pounding it with a hammer (do this in any way you desire). Then imagine sweeping and mopping away the glass and debris - refreshing the space by cleansing the smell and clearing your mind. • Focus on the mantra from the parable, "this too shall pass," because it will.
Do one thing different:	• Have a glass of water and focus mindfully on the water, the temperature, the sensation of the water as it is swallowed, the relief quenching that thirst. • Put a timer on for three minutes and focus on your breathing… breathing in for one, two, three and out … two, three. • Walk outside and eat an apple, focus on the apple until it is finished. • Remember the mantra from the parable as you breathe in and out, "this too shall pass," because it will.

	FREEDOM PRESCRIPTION FOR GAMBLING
Prescription	• Remind yourself that gambling is a fool's game! The chances of winning are very minimal. • Envision the poker machine laughing at you, or the casino attendants pointing and laughing at you, and see the person who takes your bet, gleefully and greedily rubbing their hands together, laughing at you because they know gambling is a fool's game. They know they're stealing your money for keeps and paying for their dreams with your money. • Imagine walking past them with your head held high, completely in control and with a smile that has a hint of smugness. "Not anymore…" you hear yourself say to them. • Focus on your 'wish list' for your ideal life - for example, feeling proud; being an honest person, successful and abundant; feeling calm, happy and productive; spending quality time with the people you love; holding the keys to your ideal car or house; fulfilling your dreams. • Think of the sum of money you were going to, or did use to, gamble and write down all the meaningful things you could buy for you and your family instead.

FREEDOM PRESCRIPTION FOR GAMBLING	
Do one thing different:	• Have a glass of water and focus mindfully on the water, the temperature, the sensation of the water as it is swallowed, the relief quenching that thirst. • Put a timer on for three minutes and focus on your breathing… breathing in for one, two, three and out … two, three. • Walk outside and eat an apple, focus on the apple until it is finished. • Remember the mantra from the parable as you breathe in and out, "this too shall pass," because it will.

FREEDOM PRESCRIPTION FOR DRUGS	
Prescription	• Ask the part of you that has the urge, "Is it a thought or a craving/pang?" • Tell the thought that you don't want that destructive, filthy, ugly, toxic substance in your body and imagine the thought releasing through the top of your head. • Focus your attention on remembering how bad you felt when you were coming down/off. • Focus on what you want life to be like instead.

FREEDOM PRESCRIPTION FOR DRUGS

Prescription	• Imagine two paths in front of you. The path to the left is the future the 'drug user' you could take. Imagine walking down that path and experiencing the life you would lead as a result (poverty stricken, alone, unhealthy, anxious, depressed, lacking confidence, introverted, lacking motivation, unhappy, etc). • The path to the right is the future 'drug free' you and the life you lead as a result (successful, abundant, loving life, healthy and vital, energetic, happy, enjoying great relationships). Walk both paths, which path do you choose? • Make a list of all the positive things in life that you love (for example, walking on the beach, a hug, telling someone you love that you love them, a sunrise or sunset, the birth of your first child, a special moment with your child, the last time you remember having a belly laugh, playing with a puppy, painting, listening to your favorite song, a nice bubble bath, eating your favorite food). Put your attention on two of them for 60 seconds each and smile. Feel what you feel, imagine each experience with all of your senses activated. When you think positive thoughts and smile, your brain releases endorphins and gives you an energy boost. You activate your own high!

FREEDOM PRESCRIPTION FOR DRUGS	
Do one thing different:	• Have a glass of water and focus mindfully on the water, the temperature, the sensation of the water as it is swallowed, the relief quenching that thirst. • Put a timer on for three minutes and focus on your breathing… breathing in for one, two, three and out … two, three. • Walk outside and eat an apple, focus on the apple until it is finished. • Remember the mantra from the parable as you breathe in and out, "this too shall pass," because it will.

Support Yourself

Your daily routine and daily habits in other areas of your life all add up to affect your mindset and your vibration.

- What are you listening to?
- What are you reading?
- What are you watching?
- What words do you hear yourself say?
- What emotions do you focus on?

I have clients come and see me absolutely distraught because of what they see on the news every day. You can stay informed without being bombarded. Focusing on the negative aspects of what's going on in the world can trigger the old neural pathways. Stay focused on what brings you peace, happiness, strength, kindness, good health and more.

When you become more mindful of what you focus on, what you think about and how you're reacting to the world on a daily basis, you can help yourself grow, heal, practice being peaceful and calm and, ultimately, change your life. If you practice new positive habits, you reprogram the old way of being and you also strengthen new programming, just like you would strengthen your muscles if you consistently lifted weights.

Mindfulness

Mindfulness is a very good place to start. Become aware of how much you are thinking about the past or the future and see if you can take a few moments to be present in the now. For example:

- when you take a shower, focus on being in that moment, experiencing the water, the warmth, the smells of the soap or shampoo. Think about the water running down your back, think about how you are wriggling your toes. Experience the warmth all over your body.
- Or be present while enjoying a cup of coffee. Hold the cup and be aware of the smell, the heat on your hands, the taste on your lips.

Being present in moments like these can bring you a great sense of peace and tranquility and can deliver lots of feel-good endorphins too.

Meditation and self-hypnosis

Regularly listen to self-hypnosis audios focused on your specific goals and aspirations. Meditation is a good way to practice mindfulness and being present. In this age of the internet, there are so many resources at your fingertips.

Read, listen and tune in to material that serves you. Choose content that is nurturing and positive that will help you grow and inspire you.

My Strangler Fig Moment...The Tipping Point

Picture this...

It's 1997, I'm 22 years old and it's the end of summer. I'm lying in bed at 7am drinking cask red wine out of a plastic tumbler. I have never felt so alone.

I had recently moved into a rented share house in Cape Town, South Africa, and the other occupants in the house were lovely, but all were more than 30 years older than me.

By that stage of my life, feeling alone in the world was nothing new. This particular 'aloneness', however, had hit me very hard.

I'd met someone special while living in the United Kingdom and, after some time, I had moved to Cape Town to be with him. His parents had given him an ultimatum to break it off with me. It turned out that this boy had no backbone and I found myself alone again.

Not only was I hurting from the rejection, but I was also stuck alone in a foreign country on a temporary visa. I was at a loss as to how I would raise enough money for a one-way ticket home to New Zealand.

With hindsight, it ended up being a blessing in disguise. However, at the time, I was devastated.

Looking back, I can see the pain of this particular rejection at the tender age of 22 was intensified because it had triggered the decades of loneliness, abandonment and rejection that I had experienced all of my life. It came crashing down on me in a wave of pain.

CHAPTER 10: TAKE CONTROL AND GAIN FREEDOM

Earlier in the book, I mentioned I had been taken from my mother and put into a children's home at the age of two. After living in the home for a few months, I was placed in the care of my paternal grandparents. I had a lonely childhood and my grandmother usually cast her anger and rage towards me.

My grandfather was the one bright spot in my childhood, but he sadly passed away when I was 10, after I had watched him become ravaged by cancer over a two-year period. By that stage, my grandmother was elderly and so wrapped up in her grief that she left me all alone to fend for myself.

I lived with my father from the age of 11 to 14, but he was an abusive man who left me in his dilapidated home alone much of the time. I was so grateful when my Aunt Ricci rescued me when I was 14.

My relief and safety were again short lived when, on my last visit to New Zealand, Aunt Ricci had a violent alcohol-fueled rage, screamed a barrage of verbal abuse at me and kicked me out of the home. She became yet another person in the long list of people who'd taught me about abuse and rejection. It was many years before I heard from my Aunt Ricci again.

Lying in that bed in Cape Town, clutching my tumbler of wine, I was overcome with grief, rejection and despair. It was the tipping point.

You see, there had always been two parts to me.

Part 1: This part was full of fear, abandonment and loneliness. It coped by building a wall around me and making me numb and detached. This was the part that could easily succumb to the generational trauma of abandonment and addiction. This was the part that grappled with that tumbler of wine on that grief-stricken morning.

But there was another part to me.

Part 2: This part had been with me even as a child. This part was creative and entrepreneurial, she dreamed of a better life where she was successful and had people to love who also loved her.

This part of me was always coming up with ideas and projects:

- I produced a monthly magazine
- I started a small business in the neighborhood
- I did odd jobs in the spirit of success
- I was the girl at Brownies and Girl Guides who had three times as many badges on her sash as the other girls, and
- The one who always sold the most Girl Guide cookies

This part of me threw myself into everything I did with passion. At age 10, I had my first job collecting money for the newspaper round. This was the part of me that always had an unexplained burning desire… for what? I wasn't sure.

Perhaps it was a desire to be free.

Lying on that bed with the cask of wine at my side, I knew both parts of me were at their lowest point. I was at war with myself. I always had been.

That morning … I looked at the clock as it clicked past 7.01am. That was the moment I decided that the part of me that had yearned for a healthy and successful life - the part that wanted to be strong, confident and abundant - was the part of me that would win the battle. That was the very moment, the tipping point, that I gave the strong part of me all of my focus, all of my love and attention.

Rather than succumb and let dependency and abandonment wrap around me and numb me with addiction like the strangler fig, I decided to peel the loneliness and pain away and find my strength and determination to fight back. I took back control of my life. I broke off the roots of the strangler fig that had begun to sprout and I picked off any remaining seeds.

I put down the tumbler of wine, threw away the cask and stood tall to rise above the trauma and generational addiction.

I consciously rooted my feet to the ground and became the tree trunk that survived the threat of the strangler fig.

The beauty of this strength that grew from this moment left me with a deep understanding and compassion for both my mother, Natalie, and my Aunt Ricci. I see them both now without pain and without judgement. Both women were incredibly talented and beautiful souls, but they never knew how to find the strength to rise above the trauma that life had thrown at them. They never chose to peel away their strangler figs.

This life experience is what I truly believe helps me connect with the many clients I help. I understand their hard choices, I get the pain, because I've seen it from the inside too.

> I found love and acceptance, in me. I found love and acceptance all around me. I found a way to stand strong, tall and proud in my own skin...you can too!

If one person can peel the strangler fig away, so can another and another. If one person can learn the skills to stand in their strength and say yes to life and no to addictive substances and habits, then so too can another and another.

Perhaps it's time to stop asking 'How?' and start asking 'Who'? - who has the skills to help you achieve what you want? Who has the compassion to understand the challenge and provide the proven steps for you to take?

◇◇

Perhaps it's time to stop asking 'How?' and start asking 'Who'? - who has the skills to help you achieve what you want?

◇◇

Please reach out and ask for help. We do not need to walk this path alone when there are others who have already fought the battle and won, when there are others who can hold your hand through the steps while you find your freedom from addiction too.

> Please reach out to me - Juanita.activatehypnotherapy@gmail.com - wherever you are in the world and whatever stage of your journey to freedom and strength you are at. You are not meant to do it alone. It doesn't matter how often you've tried before, what matters is that you do so again. You get to choose.

You are not alone

Whether I'm working with a client in my clinic, or reaching out through these pages to you, I want to stress that I am the 'post-treatment support hotline'. My 5-Step System is the start of your freedom. I'm here to support you beyond and into your future.

If you require extra support, or would simply like to speak with me personally, you can reach me via my
website: www.activatehypnotherapy.com.au or
Facebook: https://www.facebook.com/activatehypnotherapy

> **Free Resources**
>
> You can also access a free self-hypnosis audio to release yourself from your personal strangler fig. Download the audio free from www.isitahabitoranaddiction.com/resources

The Free Audio

'Break Free from Cravings'
This audio takes you on the journey to set yourself free of the strangler fig that has been attached to you, whatever substance, behavior, thought or reaction you've been in the habit of doing. And now, you're seeking complete freedom.

Love and light to you,

Juanita Smith

PS. Throughout the book, I introduced you to various moments and people who have impacted my life. If you are at all curious, I have included a mini photo album here.

When my Publisher asked me to put together these photos to represent the moments and people of my life that had impacted my choices, I realized a number of things:

1. These people, their stories, their highs and lows, became the wisdom that makes up the rich tapestry of who I have become.
2. I realized that I did not have many photos to choose from. Of the rare occasions I got to visit my mother or see my brother after we were separated, I only found a couple of images.
3. Although my life was surrounded by trauma and addiction from an early age, it is not the experiences I was born into that defined me, it was what I chose to do with those experiences that makes me who I am today. I think I did okay!

What defines you?

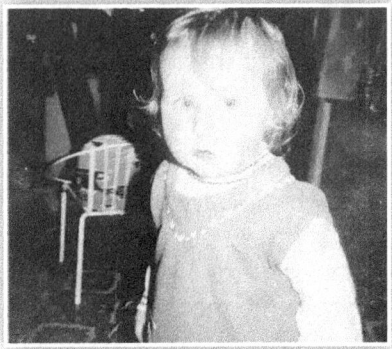

Me aged 2, just before I was taken from my mother and placed into a home.

My brother Terry and I on a rare visiting day, separated after we were put in the home, we hardly got to see each other.

I didn't get to see my mother often after we were separated. This is one of the rare visits.

My Grandparents took me out of the home and I lived with them until I was 10, when my darling Grandfather died, my grandmother couldn't continue to look after me.

My mother, Aunt Ricci and Aunt Helen, all grew up in a tough environment surrounded by trauma and addiction.

The years I lived with my father were stressful. This is me in his backyard.

My travelling years overseas. Alcohol was a big part of my life by then.

My mother and I barely knew each other, a rare moment together at my brother Terry's wedding when I was 16 years old.

My darling granddad died when I was 10, my safety once again was threatened.

Rejected again, only this time, rejection became the tipping point to choose me over alcohol and poor relationships.

Me aged 25 getting it together at last.

A rare photo of my mother before she died. Here she holds one of my two children, Amelia

My big brother Terry and I building a relationship as adults.

My amazing family today, my husband Ronnie, and our two girls, Amelia and Ruby. I am blessed.

ACKNOWLEDGEMENTS

To my partner in life, Ronnie, who has given me unwavering support over the past 21 years, no matter what crazy venture I pursued! Thank you for doing more than your fair share of the cooking, cleaning and looking after the girls for many long periods of time (especially while I've been writing this book) but, most importantly, thank you for always believing in me. Lots of love to you and our daughters, Amelia and Ruby. Your love has helped me to open my heart and heal.

To my mentor Leonie O'Connell for your generosity and wisdom. You have taught me so much and I wouldn't be where I am today without you. Thank you from the bottom of my heart.

To my publisher, editor and mentor Maggie Wilde who always overdelivers with enthusiasm and a sense of fun. Your talent, dedication and encouragement has exceeded all my expectations and the outcome is bigger and better than I could ever have imagined.

To Trish Walker who always shows up with a smile and a kind word. Thank you for your hard work and for always being there.

To Mark Hunt for writing the foreword for my book and your commitment to the cause. Thank you for your generosity and the laughs.

To my cousin Shayne P Carter for all of your support. Despite being super busy, you took the time to review, and provide valuable input and advice and I'm so grateful.

To my dear friend Rosalyn Paterson for taking the time out of your hectic schedule to lend a helping hand in the proofing stages.

To everyone else who was involved in this book by either sharing their expert knowledge, reviewing the book, or sharing their own personal journey of overcoming addiction. Thank you, thank you, thank you!

REFERENCES AND RECOMMENDED READING

Barnes, Jimmy. Working Class Boy: A memoir of running away. Harper Collins 2016.

Barnes, Jimmy. Working Class Man: A memoir of running out of time. Harper Collins 2017.

Brand, Russell. Recovery: Freedom From Our Addictions. Henry Holt and Company 2017.

Carter, Shayne. Dead People I Have Known. Victoria University Press 2019.

Dispenza, Joe. Breaking the Habit of Being Yourself: How to Lose Your Mind and Create a New One. Hay House Inc. 2013.

Hunt, Mark and Ben McKelvey. Born To Fight: The "Super Samoan" Heavyweight's Unforgettable Story of Sadness, Hope, Pride, Honour and Triumph. Hachette Australia 2015

Miller, Richard J. Drugged: The Science and Culture Behind Psychotropic Drugs. Oxford University Press 2014.

Smith, Hilda M. Not By A Long Chalk. Hot Metal Press 2007.

1. Adapted from an article by Amanda Hamos and Margaretha Haglundb, From Social Taboo to "torch of freedom": the marketing of cigarettes to women FREE. BMJ Journals Vol., 9, Issue 1 https://tobaccocontrol.bmj.com/content/9/1/3
2. *Adapted from an article in 1914-1918 Online International Encyclopedia of the first World War Version 1.0|Last updated 23 May 2018 Smoking and Cigarette Consumption by Michael Reeve 23 May 2018* https://encyclopedia.1914-1918-online.net/article/smoking_and_cigarette_consumption

www.worldpopulationreview.com

McLeod, Saul. Pavlov's Dogs, Simply Psychology 2018

Gowin Ph.D., Joshua. 7 Reasons We Can't Turn Down Fast Food, Psychology Today, August 8, 2011

Oktoberfest, Wikipedia, the free encyclopedia

Weiser, Kathy. Poker Alice – Famous Frontier Gambler, Legends of America, October 2019

Crowley, Michael. The Whale That Nearly Drowned The Donald, Politico Magazine, February 14, 2016

Redd, Wyatt. Vin Mariani – The Cocaine-Laced Wine Loved by Popes, Thomas Edison, And Ulysses S. Grant. All That's Interesting, January 31, 2018

McCann, Erin. Coke Contests and Chugging Whiskey: The Drug-Fueled Ballad Of John Belushi. Weird History, June 14, 2019

Hazlett, Courtney. Today, December 11, 2012

Freeman, Hadley. The Tragic Legacy of John Belushi. The Guardian, January 11, 2019

Rough, Lisa. Jamaica's Cannabis Roots: The History of Ganja on the Island. Leafly, May 14, 2015

Simms, Sara. History of the Rave Scene: How DJs Built Modern Dance Music. DJ Tech Tools, December 19, 2013

Nowak, Laurel. Can Drugs Trigger Serious Mental Illness? Bridges to Recovery, January 8, 2019

MEET THE CONTRIBUTORS

Mark "Super Samoan" Hunt
UFC Champion (the real-life Rocky)

Mark very kindly provided the foreword to this book and I am very grateful for his commitment as I know how busy he is. Mark is the best-selling author of Born to Fight, and he is the UFC champion (the real-life Rocky).

Facebook: www.facebook.com/therealmarkhunt

Dr Christopher John Hunt PhD
Clinical Psychologist

Dr Christopher John Hunt is a registered clinical psychologist working at the University of Sydney's Gambling Treatment Clinic. He completed his PhD in social psychology at the University of Sydney in 2012. His PhD research was entitled "Links Between Masculinity Threats and Increased Gender Conformity: An Investigation of New Empirical Directions, Process and Individual Differences" and focused on the maintenance of gender role norms. He previously completed a Bachelor of Science (Advanced) (Honours) from the University of Sydney and a Master of Psychology (Clinical) from the University of New South Wales. Dr Hunt also completed a research fellowship at the University of Trieste (Italy) in 2014, and spent some time visiting the University of Padua (Italy) in 2012.

Dr Hunt has testified before both federal and state parliamentary committees on gambling, has been extensively quoted on gambling in local, national and international media, and has written several pieces on gambling for lay audiences. He is responsible for providing clinical supervision to intern psychologists at the clinic and other mental health practitioners working in the field of problem gambling.

https://sydney.edu.au/brain-mind/patient-services/gambling-treatment-clinic.html

Josette Freeman
Senior National Program Manager at SMART Recovery Australia

Josette Freeman has an extensive background in nursing and specialized in Pediatric Oncology, Counseling and Community Development. She specializes in the field of Alcohol and Other Drugs for SMART Recovery Australia in the capacity of the Senior National Program Coordinator. She travels extensively throughout Australia and New Zealand to teach organizations and individuals about the SMART Recovery program.

Josette is the author of the *SMART Recovery Facilitator* manual and the *SMART Recovery Participants* for the Australian audience. She co-authored the *BeSMART Family and Friends* manual with Angela Argent. Josette also worked in collaboration with Aboriginal workers to develop the *Aboriginal and Torres Strait Islander edition of the SMART Recovery* manual.

www.smartrecoveryaustralia.com.au

Julian Docherty
Drug and Alcohol Rehabilitation Expert with The Salvation Army

Julian has worked in the drug and alcohol field for over five years, four of which were spent working in residential rehabilitation centers and the remaining time in out-client drug and alcohol support services. His background and training are in mental health, community services and lived experience. For support relating to alcohol, drugs and gambling, please log an enquiry at the website link for Salvation Army and their service will make contact with you.

www.salvationarmy.org.au

MEET THE AUTHOR

Juanita Smith operates three busy hypnotherapy clinics in Sydney, Australia, and specializes in addiction and trauma. Her passion and compassion to help clients achieve freedom from addiction comes from a place of personal experience and deep understanding.

Juanita has personally helped thousands of clients with her proven techniques. She is an author and trainer for the Sydney-based Academy of Therapeutic Hypnosis and is passionate about how powerful hypnosis is to overcome addiction and trauma.

Training and Online Courses Available:

Trainer for The Academy of Therapeutic Hypnosis offering:

- ▶ Certification in Clinical Hypnotherapy and specialist Practitioner training in:
- ▶ Quit Smoking & Other Addictions
- ▶ Desired Weight Loss & Virtual Gastric Band Hypnosis
- ▶ Anxiety & Panic Attacks

MEET THE AUTHOR

Online Course by Juanita Smith:

▶ Practitioner - Advanced Stop Smoking & Vaping Masterclass

▶ Practitioner - Stop Smoking & Vaping Mentoring Program

Books and articles by Juanita Smith

▶ Is It a Habit or An Addiction?

▶ Empowering Stories from Female Leaders Who Said YNot

▶ YMag July, 2020

Contact
Website: www.activatehypnotherapy.com.au
Email: Juanita.activatehypnotherapy@gmail.com

Free Resources
www.isitahabitoranaddiction.com/resources

WHAT OTHERS HAVE TO SAY...

"This book gives me hope that there is a plan or a strategy that can form a pathway out of addiction. For anyone facing their own battle with addiction, this book is a shining light to clarity and hope for the future. And, for any practitioner who would like more insight into how to help clients, this is a must read!"

Annette Marshall
Natural Therapist, NSW Australia

"Juanita's work changes lives. I recommend this book to anyone working with addiction. She grew up surrounded by addiction and abuse. For many people, this could have had a very negative impact on her life, but Juanita chose to use her personal experience as an impetus to help others in the most profound way – freeing them of their addictive patterns and giving them back their life.

This book outlines the steps she takes to bring people back from a place where they feel hopeless and helpless to a place where they are free again."

Leonie O'Connell, Principal, Academy of Therapeutic Hypnosis Clinical Hypnotherapist and Trainer
www.aoth.com.au

WHAT OTHERS HAVE TO SAY...

"A clear-eyed, compassionate analysis of the nature of addiction that also lays out a plan for a happier, more fulfilled life. Juanita writes with the authority and understanding that comes from both personal and professional experience with addiction, making her account logical, empathetic and thoughtful."

Shayne P Carter, Musician and Author
Award winning Author and Member of the New Zealand Music Hall of Fame

'Is It A Habit or an Addiction?' is a very engaging and relatable read. The stories, which are haunting, hard hitting and heartwarming all at once, are weaved in around the expert advice and proven processes to provide a wonderful helping hand to someone struggling with addiction. The invitation to gain clarity and a clear step-by-step action plan is a warm embrace and a guiding hand to see a way forward out of where they are stuck. I'd recommend it to anyone struggling with addiction."

Gretel Khan
A Coach for Newly Separated Parents Looking to Survive and Thrive.

www.greteljane.com.au

www.ingramcontent.com/pod-product-compliance
Lightning Source LLC
Chambersburg PA
CBHW071629080526
44588CB00010B/1326